Richard Chin has written a guide to the Christian life as presented in Colossians that is—like Paul's letter—clear and simple, pithy and punchy. The book is compact but powerful. Theology and practical matters are both presented accurately from the text, and steeped in Richard's own experience of following Christ for years and helping others to do the same. This book is a model for people in their own Bible reading, for small group leaders, and even for preachers as they prepare messages from Colossians. I highly commend it.

Mark Dever
Pastor, Capitol Hill Baptist Church, Washington DC
President, 9marks.org

Richard Chin's excellent guide to Colossians is written with characteristic pithiness and clarity. He explains the text of Colossians in a way that is understandable and readable. His careful illustration and acute observation enable the reader to see just how and where the teaching of Colossians applies today. Above all else, this book directs the reader to the Lord Jesus Christ in all his fullness. This is what makes the book so valuable. It did me good, and reading it refreshed me in my love for Jesus and appreciation of who he is, and all that he has done.

William Taylor
Rector, St Helen's, Bishopsgate, London

Richard Chin has given us an engagingly written book, both respectful of God's word and also continuously applied in a deeply personal way. It helps us all to learn from Colossians.

Peter Jensen
Former Anglican Archbishop of Sydney
General Secretary, GAFCON

I met Richard several years ago at a student ministry conference. I was immediately impressed by his clear, careful and winsome exposition of Scripture. Those same qualities are on display in this excellent treatment of Colossians. Richard offers us personal stories, lessons from history, present-day application, and (most importantly) faithful teaching rooted in words of the Bible. This book is a terrific resource for seekers, new believers and long-time Christians alike.

Kevin DeYoung
Senior Pastor, Christ Covenant Church, Matthews, NC
Assistant Professor of Systematic Theology, Reformed Theological Seminary, Charlotte, NC

This book has helped me to see Jesus Christ more clearly from the Bible. Whenever *that* happens, as Christians all over the world discover, God speaks straight into your sinful heart, then comforts you with his forgiveness, helps you by his Spirit to grow in mature Christlikeness, *and* prepares you for the hard road ahead as we follow our crucified Lord to glory.

Richard has turned his series of talks on Colossians into a book that is so readable, you can almost hear him delivering each chapter. Your time in this book is worth it to be captivated by Christ!

Bronwyn Windsor
Lay ministry leader, Sydney

This is a delightful book—read it and savour it! Not only has Richard Chin gained a profound grasp on the rich letter to the Colossians, he has clearly lived it. This is clear, warm-hearted, searingly applied teaching which will both lift us up and bring us down to size, as it presents Christ to us on every page, in order to present us mature in Christ. I cannot recommend *Captivated by Christ* highly enough.

Gary Millar
Principal, Queensland Theological College
Co-author, *Saving Eutychus*

A clear, fresh, sparkling commentary, filled with helpful practical application, which gets to the heart of the apostle Paul's letter—highlighting Jesus Christ's majestic unique-ness and calling all his followers to flesh out his lordship in every sphere of life.

Lindsay Brown
Director, FEUER (Fellowship of Evangelists in the Universities of Europe)
Former General Secretary, International Fellowship of Evangelical Students

I was immediately drawn to *Captivated by Christ* by Richard's warm and winsome writing style. His engaging illustra-tions give a velvety softness to the hammer that pounds the rich and deep truths of Colossians into our soul. This is a treasure of a book, with helpful sidebars and penetrating questions for small group study. It's a joy to recommend.

J. Mack Stiles
Pastor, Erbil International Baptist Church, Iraq
Author, *Marks of the Messenger*

Captivated by Christ

Seeing Jesus clearly in the book of Colossians

Richard Chin

Captivated by Christ

Seeing Jesus clearly in the book of Colossians

Richard Chin

matthiasmedia
SYDNEY · YOUNGSTOWN

Matthias Media
(St Matthias Press Ltd ACN 067 558 365)
Email: info@matthiasmedia.com.au
Internet: www.matthiasmedia.com.au
Please visit our website for current postal and telephone contact information.

Matthias Media (USA)
Email: sales@matthiasmedia.com
Internet: www.matthiasmedia.com
Please visit our website for current postal and telephone contact information.

ISBN 978 1 925424 49 2

Cover design and typesetting by Lankshear Design.

Gratefully dedicated to my wife and prayer partner, Jeanette, and my children, Rachel, Naomi, Grace and Thomas, and in memory of my late wife, Bronwyn, who is now at home with Jesus.

"Not to us, O LORD, not to us, but to your name give glory" (Psalm 115:1)

Contents

Introduction

*I*n essence, this book began the day my life was turned on its head.

It was July 1983 at a student conference when the speaker asked, "Is Jesus number one in your life?" I knew he was a good number two or three. But he was not number one. Sometime that week, I joyfully received Jesus as my Lord.

Since then, I have journeyed as a son, a father, a widower, a husband (twice over), a church member, a worker, and, above all, as a great sinner with a great Saviour.

But no verses of Scripture describe my life's desire more closely than Colossians 2:6-7:

> Therefore, as you received Christ Jesus the Lord, so walk in him, rooted and built up in him and established in the faith, just as you were taught, abounding in thanksgiving.

This is what it means to be "mature in Christ" (1:28). But such maturity must involve a clear vision of the Jesus we receive as Lord. Sadly, this clarity can be blurred not only by deceptive teaching, but also by the air that we breathe. I wonder whether, like me, you have felt the allure of material gain, the appeal of career advancement, the pull of pride, the draw of sexual temptation, the charm of becoming more comfortable, the claim of personal rights in relationships or even a fascination with religious practices—all of which prevent us from seeing Christ clearly.

This is the same air that the Colossians breathed in the first century. That's why the New Testament letter bearing their name is so worthy of meditation and prayer. The apostle Paul gives you a gloriously clear view of Christ and how to walk in him. And the book in your hands is an attempt to apply his words from Colossians 1:28:

> Him we proclaim, warning everyone and teaching everyone with all wisdom, that we may present everyone mature in Christ.

My overriding concern is to present you "mature in Christ" by proclaiming Jesus from the pages of Colossians. And, as we work systematically through the letter, this will involve as much warning as it does teaching. There are sidebars with further thoughts, discussion questions for more reflection, and ideas for thanksgiving and prayer to bring before our Father after each chapter.

But please ensure that you meditate far more deeply on the New Testament book of Colossians itself than on anything in this book.

No New Testament letter has shaped my life and ministry more than Colossians. As such, this book began when I first received Christ Jesus as my Lord. But *writing* this book began as a series of seven sermons preached at the CMS

Summer School in Katoomba, NSW, Australia, in January 2018. The content of these pages substantially captures what was preached. I am indebted to my wife, Jeanette, for looking over my original sermons, and to Geoff Robson for helping me especially modify them into this book.

May you cherish Christ for his glory in the pages that follow.

1 | The gospel of Christ

*H*ave you ever received mail from someone that you don't know? When that happens, it's usually not very exciting—a discount pizza voucher, a bill or your local elected official telling you how wonderful he or she is.

But in the first century, a fairly unremarkable and unimpressive group of people received a letter from someone they didn't know: a man named Paul, writing his letter to the Colossians.

This group of people met regularly in someone's house—just an ordinary group of people meeting as Christians. They wouldn't have had a slick children's programme or parking attendants or beautifully designed handouts or a band with professionally trained musicians. But they probably sang. They would have read the Old Testament Scriptures, prayed together, and sought to encourage each other as followers of Jesus Christ.

One day, this letter arrived—probably delivered by two men named Tychicus and Onesimus. But this letter wasn't like most of the junk mail that passes through our letterboxes. It was a letter of such importance that it had to be read aloud, pored over, discussed, analyzed, and preserved. So imagine someone unrolling a scroll as a hush comes over the expectant Colossians, then reading out those opening words:

> Paul, an apostle of Christ Jesus by the will of God, and
>   Timothy our brother,
>   To the saints and faithful brothers in Christ at
>   Colossae:
>   Grace to you and peace from God our Father.
>   (1:1-2)

Who was Timothy?

Timothy was one of Paul's protégés and closest colleagues in gospel ministry. He joined Paul on his second missionary journey (Acts 16-20), was sent to the church at Corinth to help them resolve problems (1 Cor 4:17, 16:10), and served as a leader of the church in Ephesus (1 Tim 4:12). They were so close that Paul called Timothy "my true child in the faith" (1 Tim 1:2), and he wrote Timothy two letters—1 and 2 Timothy—to instruct him on how to shape his gospel ministry.

Since he is mentioned in 1:1, did Timothy co-author the letter? Throughout Colossians, it is much more common for the first person singular to be used (e.g. 1:23-2:5, 4:3b-18), with the first person plural only appearing occasionally (e.g. 1:3-14, 4:3a).

Therefore, it seems best to view Paul as the sole author of the letter. However, he was keen to convey just how closely he worked with Timothy—particularly to show that they were mutually encouraged by the Colossians, and that they were mutually committed to praying for them.

Paul had never met these Colossian Christians. Apart from knowing a few people like Tychicus, Onesimus and Epaphras, he'd never even seen them face to face. It was Epaphras, not Paul, who had preached the gospel to them.

So why does Paul write to this particular unimpressive, unremarkable group of people? And what does this letter have to do with us today?

The answer to that question starts with knowing the author. Paul introduces himself as an 'apostle'—literally, a 'sent one'—of Christ Jesus, who chose and sent Paul to be his ambassador. So this letter arrived with the royal stamp of approval. Paul is the official envoy of the King, representing Christ himself.

But unlike the original 12 apostles, who were sent to preach the good news of Jesus to the Jews, Paul was especially sent to the Gentiles. Actually, the word 'Gentiles' is much too weak to capture the scope of Paul's ministry. Paul was especially sent to 'the nations'. He was God's chosen instrument to take the momentous news of Jesus to 'the ends of the earth'—to people from every tribe and nation on earth. As such, even though he had never met them, Paul was the God-appointed apostle to the Colossians, just as he was to the Corinthians and the Ephesians and so many others. He's my apostle. And, if you're a Gentile, he's your apostle.

The risen Jesus sent Paul especially as the *suffering* apostle to the nations. As we'll see throughout this book, part of Paul's role involved "filling up what is lacking in Christ's afflictions" (1:24) and 'struggling' for all God's people, even those he hadn't seen face to face (2:1). At the very end of the letter, we learn that he was in chains as he wrote (4:18). Their apostle, our apostle, was the *suffering* apostle to the nations.

So we have Paul, the official envoy of King Jesus, writing personally to the Colossians from his prison cell in his role as the royal ambassador to the nations. And he endures great suffering for them.

This is a letter that deserves our attention.

Who are "the saints"?

In Colossians, as in other New Testament letters like Ephesians and 1 Peter, the word 'saints' is generally reserved for Jewish Christians, but is sometimes broadened out to include Gentile Christians. New Testament scholar Lionel Windsor brilliantly captures a key nuance:

> "The saints" in Ephesians doesn't just mean "Jewish Christians", and it doesn't just mean "all Christians". That's too static. The phrase "the saints" is used to make a point about the dynamic movement of holiness from Israel to the nations through the gospel of Christ. So "the saints" are firstly the early Jewish apostolic community, and then all those who believe in Christ—and this dynamic movement matters.[1]

This "dynamic movement of holiness" also captures the meaning of 'saints' in Colossians. In 1:2, "the saints" includes all the Jewish and Gentile Christians in Colossae who together have this holy status. But in 1:26-27, Paul clearly distinguishes "the saints" from "the Gentiles" as he uses the terms in the context of salvation history:

> ...the mystery hidden for ages and generations but now revealed to his saints. **To them** [i.e. to the saints] God

[1] 'Ephesians & Colossians: Jews, Gentiles, and the Apostolic Mission', *lionelwindsor.net*, 2017 (viewed 19 December 2018): www.lionelwindsor.net/2018/01/02/christs-mission-israel-nations/. See also his *Reading Ephesians and Colossians after Supersessionism: Christ's Mission Through Israel to the Nations*, Wipf & Stock, Eugene, OR, 2017.

chose to make known how great among **the Gentiles** are the riches of the glory of this mystery, which is Christ in you, the hope of glory.

Whatever we conclude about Paul's audience, the key idea is clearly their holy status before God. But working hard to understand the nuances of Scripture is always worth the effort. It's like watching TV in ultra-high definition as opposed to just high definition—grasping this nuance will help us understand Paul's apostolic mission more clearly as we work through the letter.

Gospel-shaped lives: faith, love and hope

So why exactly does Paul write to these people that he's never met? First, he writes to express his gratitude for their gospel-shaped lives:

> We always thank God, the Father of our Lord Jesus Christ, when we pray for you, since we heard of your faith in Christ Jesus and of the love that you have for all the saints, because of the hope laid up for you in heaven. (1:3-5a)

Even from his prison cell, Paul had heard about their gospel-shaped lives: their faith, hope, and love. It's no surprise to see Paul using this famous triad to describe the Colossians.

Let's not glide too quickly over these verses. Firstly, note that the Colossians had *faith* in Jesus. They trusted Jesus as the Christ, the King who ruled all kings. They put all their weight on him. They depended on Jesus as the pulsating centre of their lives. So Paul thanked God that they trusted Jesus, and not Caesar, as their ultimate King. He thanked God that they derived their identity, their value and their status not from any earthly authority, but from Jesus.

It is worth pondering what 'authority' we look to or trust as we seek to derive our identity. Do we place our faith in our government to identify as citizens or in our employers to identify as employees or in our friendship circle to identify as 'cool' or in our family to identify as 'approved'?

Another way to discover what we see as the source of our identity is to ask: where do our private thoughts habitually flow when nothing else demands our attention? What would your private thoughts reveal? Could it be a desire for the dream career? Or the dream home? Or the special relationship?[2]

Could one of these things, or something else, inadvertently offer an authoritative identity in which we trust? Please remember that, if you're a Christian, your identity arises ultimately from your faith in Jesus Christ. And Paul gives thanks because, for the Colossians, the gospel generated this kind of deep-seated faith.

Second, Paul gives thanks that the gospel also generated their *love* for all the saints. If "the saints" includes Jewish Christians in salvation history, it's small wonder that Paul thanks God for this too. After all, in Jesus' day, the Jewish community used to equate being a 'Gentile' with being a sinner. The gospel changed all that. But having generated their faith, the gospel also kindled the Colossians' love for their Jewish brothers and sisters, despite the long history of enmity between them.

---

2 For further reflection, see Timothy Keller, *Counterfeit Gods: The Empty Promises of Money, Sex, and Power, and the Only Hope that Matters*, Penguin, New York, 2011.

This is radical. In today's terms, it's like Arab Christians embracing American Christians as family. I remember being at a conference when an Arab Christian, dressed in traditional Arab clothing, stood on stage in front of several hundred people. He was joined on stage by my dear friend Mack Stiles, an American brother who had helped pioneer a new gospel work in the Middle East. The Arab put his arm around Mack and declared, "This is my hero". This is the power of the gospel—kindling love where there would otherwise be division and enmity.

Look how Paul describes the Colossians' love: "[Epaphras] is a faithful minister of Christ on your behalf and has made known to us your love *in the Spirit*" (1:7b-8). Their love for the saints is a God-empowered, Spirit-saturated, supernatural love.

Don't ever take for granted the love that God's people have for one another. Don't ever be content to see God's people living with a lack of love among one another. After all, Jesus himself said that all people will know we're his disciples "if you have love for one another" (John 13:35).

Loving when it's hard

Is there a Christian brother or sister whom, for some reason, you find particularly difficult to love? How might Paul's words about love (his thanks for the Gentile Christians loving the Jewish Christians) shape your approach to this person?

But why did the Colossians have faith in Jesus and love for their Jewish Christian brothers and sisters? Because of their heavenly *hope*. Verse 5 tells us that their faith and their love exist "*because of* the hope laid up for you in heaven".

Hope is anticipation—a looking forward to something. Hope is what drives us on in life, and is even more powerful than fear. Hope gives us a reason to live. Many people who survived Hitler's concentration camps later said that hope sustained them, even though they had no guarantee that they would survive.

As Christians, we have a hope that preserves all this forward-looking anticipation with assurance. That's why Paul can describe our hope as being "laid up in heaven". Heaven, the place "where neither moth nor rust destroys and where thieves do not break in and steal" (Matt 6:20). Heaven, where we have an inheritance that is "imperishable, undefiled, and unfading" (1 Pet 1:4). This is guaranteed.

Can you see the power of this hope? It's no wonder that Christians down through the ages have known how to endure through suffering, and even how to die well.

My first wife, Bronwyn, died well. She passed away on Easter Sunday in 2013 after a painful battle with pancreatic cancer. But she never lost her hope. She even wrote an article titled, 'Thank God for cancer'. People were shocked by that. How do you thank God for cancer? Bronwyn knew that her sovereign Lord had assured her of her eternity, and that even cancer in this life was ultimately for her good and for his glory. Hope makes that possible.

Can you see why Paul overflows with gratitude as he writes from a prison cell? Because this seemingly unimpressive, unremarkable, rag-tag bunch of people that he had never even met *trusted* Jesus, *loved* their former enemies, and lived lives shaped by a *hope* secured in heaven.

The gospel and its fruit

Paul then tells us how the Colossians came to hear of this hope:

> Of this you have heard before in the word of the truth, the gospel, which has come to you, as indeed in the whole world it is bearing fruit and increasing— as it also does among you, since the day you heard it and understood the grace of God in truth, just as you learned it from Epaphras our beloved fellow servant. (1:5b-7a)

The Colossians heard the gospel as "the word of truth" and as "the grace of God in truth" from the lips of Epaphras.

The gospel is news—an announcement, a message. Notice the verbs that Paul uses to describe what happened: they "heard", they "learned", and they "understood" this gospel. They didn't think it up themselves. They didn't philosophize on the best way to live or the best way to relate to God. They didn't hear Epaphras' message and say, "That's a good start, but how can we make the message more palatable, more relevant or more culturally acceptable?" Epaphras proclaimed the message to them; their job was simply to hear it, to learn it, and to understand what it meant for their lives.

Moreover, the gospel bore fruit. The gospel created their faith in Christ, their love for the saints, and their hope for the future. And as such, this gospel bore fruit and grew not just among them, but also "in the whole world".

Never forget that this gospel is not just for you or your church or your friends—but for the whole world. Never rob

God of his glory by having too small a vision for his gospel. The news about Jesus is the most important force in all the world, bar none. Real power does not lie with the media or our universities or our governments or armies or the Rule of Law or social justice. Nothing in this world shapes and changes lives more than the message of Jesus.

But it's so important to note that there is a difference between the *gospel* and the *fruit* of the gospel.

The gospel is the momentous news of hope and grace in Jesus Christ. The gospel is an announcement of what God has done in Jesus to draw people to himself in love. It centres on Jesus' life, death and resurrection. It centres on his victory over sin and death, on his rule and his lordship, and on his call to submit to him as our Lord and Saviour.

The gospel is about *Jesus*.

The fruit of the gospel is about *us*.

The fruit of the gospel is about our transformed lives— our faith in Jesus, our love for each other, and our good works. The gospel creates a life of love. But the life of love itself is not the gospel.

Don't get me wrong: the life of love is the necessary fruit of the gospel, and it will adorn the gospel. But it is not the gospel. It's why the popular saying, "Preach the gospel at all times; if necessary use words" is so misleading.[3] As Ligon Duncan says, it's like saying, "Feed the hungry at all times;

---

3   These words are falsely attributed to St. Francis of Assisi—founder of the Franciscan Order—and are intended to say that proclaiming the gospel by example is more virtuous than actually proclaiming it with voice. See Glenn Stanton, 'FactChecker: Misquoting Francis of Assisi', *The Gospel Coalition,* 10 July 2012 (viewed 19 December 2018): www.the gospelcoalition.org/article/factchecker-misquoting-francis-of-assisi/.

if necessary use food".[4] There is no way to preach the gospel other than with words, because the gospel is not about us and our good lives. The gospel is the message about Jesus.

If we don't grasp this, we'll never be clear in our evangelism. We're not 'gospelling' when we care for refugees in Darfur or educate the poor in Kolkata or hand out free food on a university campus—unless we also make sure that people hear the message of Jesus.

A good friend of mine, Joe Radkovic, served as a medical missionary with CMS and set up a maternity clinic in one of the poorest slums of Kenya. Under God, he used his first-class medical training to see the infant mortality rate drop from one in ten to one in 110. He did all of this because of love. God's love drove him to provide the best possible medical care for some of the poorest people in the world.

But Joe knew that caring for the poor was not evangelism. He knew it was the fruit of the gospel, not the gospel. He knew he wasn't 'gospelling' until he shared the news of Jesus. So he arranged to have a huge gospel outline painted on the walls of his clinic, and ensured that every single person who came through the clinic heard the message of Jesus.[5]

But even though the life of love is not the gospel, it still makes an extraordinary impact. And when you see a fruit-bearing life of faith, love and hope, you know that

---

4   Ligon Duncan, 'Saying, "Preach the Gospel, use words if necessary" is like saying, "Feed the hungry, use food if necessary"', Twitter, 31 October 2017, 6:54pm (viewed 27 December 2018): www.twitter. com/ligonduncan/status/925541401554759680.
5   Joe used an adapted version of the *Two Ways To Live* gospel outline (see www.twowaystolive.com).

person has heard the news through an 'Epaphras', a faithful minister, somewhere along the line. And that should make our hearts burst with thanksgiving.

Stop and think for a moment: who is the 'Epaphras' in your life? Who can you thank God for? Who has shared this gospel with you? Is it your family? Is it a Sunday School teacher, a friend or a faithful minister? We can thank God for them, just as Paul was clearly thankful for Epaphras, his "beloved fellow servant".

But let me also ask you: who are the 'Colossians' in your life? Whose lives can you thank God for—even if you haven't met them? One of my great joys is to read prayer letters from missionaries all over the world. It's a joy to learn about people reading the Bible for the first time or becoming Christians or wanting to apply the word of God to their lives. I've never met most of the people mentioned in those letters, but I can thank God for them. Every time you get a prayer letter or an email from a missionary and you pray for the people they're serving, you're praying for the 'Colossians' in your life.

Paul's gospel-shaped prayer

Paul was filled with gratitude for the way the gospel had generated faith, love and hope in the Colossians' lives, and this gratitude drove him to prayer. The opening words of verse 9 tell us not just *what* he prayed, but *why* he prayed:

> And so [more accurately, "Because of this"—because he is so grateful for the gospel fruit in their lives], from the day we heard, we have not ceased to pray for

you, asking that you may be filled with the knowledge of his will in all spiritual wisdom and understanding, so as to walk in a manner worthy of the Lord, fully pleasing to him: bearing fruit in every good work and increasing in the knowledge of God... (1:9-10)

At first glance, it seems like Paul prays for many different things in these two verses. But if we look closely, it turns out he's only really praying for one key thing: that they will be "filled with the knowledge of his will". Everything else flows out of this one core request.

But what does it mean to be "filled with the knowledge of [God's] will?" Does it mean that you can expect God to provide you with specific guidance about your personal future? Do you have "knowledge of God's will" when you know who to marry or where to live or what job to get or which course to study or where to go to church?

Now, God *may* provide you with specific, personal guidance along those lines. He's God—he can do anything he wants to. In answer to your question, "Should I marry Zedekiah?", he could write you a personal message in blazing letters across the sky: "No!"

But this kind of "knowledge of God's will" isn't what Paul has in mind here, and it's not what God promises us. Paul's focus is on what God *delights in* and what God *takes pleasure in*. It's much less about knowing what my specific future holds, and much more about knowing what will be pleasing to God.

This kind of knowledge involves, firstly, spiritual wisdom and understanding (1:9b). It's given by the same Spirit who gave the Colossians their love for all the saints.

Secondly, this kind of knowledge is in contrast to "the elemental spirits of the world" that Paul mentions in 2:8. And where can we find such wisdom and knowledge? As we read through Colossians we'll see this idea crop up in many different contexts, but for now let's jump ahead to chapter 2:

> For I want you to know how great a struggle I have for you and for those at Laodicea and for all who have not seen me face to face, that their hearts may be encouraged, being knit together in love, to reach all the riches of full assurance of understanding and the knowledge of God's mystery, which is *Christ, in whom* are hidden all the treasures of wisdom and knowledge. (2:1-3)

The answer is strikingly simple: all the treasures of wisdom and knowledge are found *in Christ*. As we'll see in the next chapter of this book, Paul is about to present us with a breathtaking picture of the majesty, the wonder, the magnificence, and the supremacy of Jesus Christ in all things.

In other words, if you want knowledge of what pleases God, and if you want spiritual wisdom and understanding, look to Jesus. As we come to see Jesus more clearly, so we will grow in knowledge, wisdom and understanding of God's will. As we see Jesus more clearly, the gospel gets bigger and bigger in our hearts. His death becomes more wonderful. His resurrection becomes more astonishing. Sin becomes more disgusting and the devil seems more evil. The restoring work of the Spirit gets mightier. The global extent of the gospel becomes more important. The connections between everything within the Bible become clearer. Our yearning for eternity becomes greater. And the love of God becomes more delightful.[6]

That's why Paul expects that this knowledge will lead God's people to "walk in a manner worthy of the Lord, fully pleasing to him", and it's why he expects that they will continue "bearing fruit in every good work and increasing in the knowledge of God" (1:10).

Paul not only thanks God for the fruit in the Colossians' lives; he also prays for more fruit! Paul's gratitude flows over into his request for more. He doesn't want the Colossians to rest on their laurels and think, "We're spiritually mature enough". There's no such thing! Paul pleads with God to give the Colossians *more* faith in Jesus, and *more* love for all the saints, and *more* understanding of the hope laid up in heaven for them. Paul is greedy for their continued growth.

In Paul's understanding, Christian life and ministry is not just meant to be problem-centred—looking around for the people who've gone off the rails and helping them to get back on track. A huge part of gospel ministry is finding the people who are, by God's grace, living the life of faith, love and hope—and praying that God will keep working in them so they might be *filled* with the knowledge of his will, *fully* pleasing to him, living with *ever more* faith, love and hope.

In verse 11, Paul then goes on to pray that God would give them power. But power for what?

If you were to ask God for power, what kind of power would it be? Power to succeed in everything you do? Power

---

6   cf. John Piper, 'Never Let the Gospel Get Smaller', *Desiring God*, 17 March 2009 (viewed 19 December 2018): www.desiringgod.org/articles/never-let-the-gospel-get-smaller.

to crush your enemies? Or maybe something more godly, like power to preach the gospel and see thousands saved? Look at the kind of power Paul prays that they'll have: "...being strengthened with all power, according to his glorious might, for *all endurance and patience with joy...*" (1:11).

Paul prays that they would be strengthened with all power *to endure*. Why is that necessary? Because living a life pleasing to the Lord will put us on a direct collision course with a world that is opposed to him—a world of darkness. If we please God, we will not please this world. And we will suffer accordingly.

This is happening more and more in Western societies, as God's people increasingly face ostracism for holding to the truth of his word. And throughout the history of the church, it's been happening in violent and frightening ways for brothers and sisters around the world.

In another letter, Paul says that "all who desire to live a godly life in Christ Jesus will be persecuted" (2 Tim 3:12). Not *some*, but *all*. And not *may* be, but *will* be. We need to remember, and we need to teach our children, that persecution is a normal part of the Christian life. And we all need God's power to endure whatever assaults come our way.

But not only will Christians suffer through persecution. We'll also suffer the effects of a broken and divided world filled with suffering, turmoil, tragedy, sin, and death. Our hearts will rightly sting as we look at the darkness of this world until Jesus returns. And yet, Paul says, we can give thanks through it all.

But what do we have to thank God for in this dark world?

...giving thanks to the Father, who has qualified you to share in the inheritance of the saints in light. He has delivered us from the domain of darkness and transferred us to the kingdom of his beloved Son, in whom we have redemption, the forgiveness of sins. (1:12-14)

We can thank God because, in his incredible kindness, he has dealt with our greatest need. Our greatest need is not to be healed from sickness, nor to experience harmony and justice in our societies, nor to see poverty eradicated, nor even to establish lasting peace with each other. Our greatest need, above all others, is to be transferred into Christ's kingdom and have our sins forgiven.

Someone somewhere once wrote, "I have learned to kiss the wave that throws me against the Rock of Ages".[7] We too can learn to kiss the wave of dark trials, because we have certain hope laid up in heaven for us. We share in the inheritance of the saints in light. We have been forgiven all our sins, because of Jesus. We have absolute security in God's Kingdom.

Can you now begin to see why this letter transformed the lives of the Colossian Christians as they read it and pored over it together? Their apostle thanked God for their gospel-generated faith, love and hope. And they heard how his gratitude ignited his unceasing prayers for them to see

---

7 These famous words are falsely attributed to Charles Spurgeon. Wherever they originated, they beautifully capture biblical truth. See '6 Quotes Spurgeon Didn't Say', *The Spurgeon Center*, 8 August 2017 (viewed 19 December 2018): www.spurgeon.org/resource-library/blog-entries/6-quotes-spurgeon-didnt-say.

Christ and his plans for the whole world more clearly, so that they could live gospel-shaped lives.

May the same be true for us as we delve deeply into the words written for us by our apostle.

Give thanks and pray

- Thank God for the apostle Paul. Pray that God would renew your mind and transform your life as you read Paul's letter to the Colossians.
- Thank God for the ways in which the gospel is bearing fruit in your life. Pray that God would enable you to grow in maturity and bear even more fruit.
- Thank God for those who have shared the gospel with you, and pray that their ministry would continue to bear fruit in the lives of many people.

Discussion questions

- Where, other than Jesus Christ, are you most tempted to seek your sense of identity?
- "The news about Jesus is the most important force in all the world, bar none." Do you agree? Why or why not?
- What resources or methods can you use to pray for "the Colossians in your life"—Christians to thank God for, even if you've never met them?
- Have you learned to "kiss the wave that throws you against the Rock of Ages"? What might help you to further develop this mindset?

2 | Clearly Christ

always get my hair cut at the same barber shop by the first available of four barbers. My personal barber shop quartet, you might say. These men are all talkers—and the longer we talk, the shorter my haircut! So the quality of my personal evangelism depends on my vanity.

My barbers' names are Craig, Jonny, Charlie and—my personal favourite—'Nudge'. And Nudge is multi-talented. He not only cuts hair; he also trains champion boxers. When he took one of his young champions to Malta to beat the living daylights out of his opponent, Nudge also visited a tattoo parlour. When he returned to Australia, he proudly showed me the masterpiece that had taken 15 hours of pain to create: an image of Jesus.

I asked Nudge why he wanted a picture of Jesus permanently inked onto his body. He replied, "I like the idea of a man who suffered for doing good". Even though Nudge is not yet living for Jesus as his Lord, Jesus' reputation is enough to attract him.

Needless to say, my hair ended up very short that day.

It's easy to be impressed or fascinated by Jesus. Who could look at this man, the most extraordinary life ever lived, and not find something compelling? Yet it's entirely possible to be fascinated or impressed or even compelled by Jesus, and yet still have a distorted view of him. It's not enough to be interested in a Jesus of our own making. We need to have faith in the *real* Jesus—the Jesus of the biblical gospel.

In the first century, there were cultural and social forces at work among the Colossians, presenting plausible-sounding arguments that made it easy to accept a distorted view of Jesus. And in the 21st century, there are powerful cultural and social forces at work that can easily distort our view of Jesus. So Paul writes one of the great passages of Scripture to help the Colossians, and to help us, see Jesus in all his splendor, his magnificence, and his breathtaking reality. Who is this Jesus revealed to us in Paul's letter?

The real Jesus

First, this Jesus is the beloved Son of the Father.

Paul has already opened his letter with these words: "Grace to you and peace from God our Father" (1:2b). Our God is Father, through and through. Everything he does, he does as the Father. He *creates* as the Father, and he *rules* as the Father. But most of all, he *loves* as the Father. In fact, Paul says that God "has qualified you to share in the inheritance of the saints in light. He has delivered us from the domain of darkness and transferred us to the kingdom of his beloved Son..." (1:12b-13).

God's very identity, his Fatherhood, is bound up with loving and delighting in his Son, which he has been doing for all eternity. God is like a fountain bursting forth and spilling over in love for his Son. And this overflowing love of the Father for his Son provides the subterranean waters that flow through Paul's majestic description of Jesus in verses 15-20.

Here's how Paul begins this extraordinary passage:

He [Jesus] is the image of the invisible God, the first-born of all creation. For by him all things were created, in heaven and on earth, visible and invisible, whether thrones or dominions or rulers or authorities—all things were created through him and for him. (1:15-16)

Did you realize that all things—literally all things, including you—were made by Jesus (more accurately 'in' Jesus), through Jesus, and for Jesus?

The overflowing love of the Father led him to create all things for his Son. But Jesus is not only the beloved Son; he is also the very agent through whom God created all things. So the Son is also the Creator. And because all things were created in, through and for Jesus, he is "the image of the invisible God".

Only Jesus is the perfect, visible representation of God. Adam and Eve were meant to visibly represent God as his image-bearers, but they failed. The nation of Israel was meant to represent God, but she failed. And we are meant to represent God, but we fail over and over again.

In 1954, an artist named Graham Sutherland was commissioned to paint a full-length portrait of Sir Winston Churchill, arguably Great Britain's most famous Prime Minister, on the occasion of Churchill's 80th birthday. Churchill wanted the portrait to portray the image of the office of Prime Minister—to capture him with a sense of gravitas and splendor.

But the final portrait proved to be a long way from the image Churchill desired. It showed him sitting slumped over in a simple wooden chair, bearing a quizzical scowl, surrounded by bleak and wintry tones. Churchill thought it made him "look like a down-and-out drunk who has been picked out of the gutter in the Strand".[8] Ironically, Mrs Churchill allegedly confessed it was "really quite alarmingly like him".[9] But, ultimately, both Churchill and his wife despised the portrait. So instead of being hung in the houses of Parliament as a lasting monument to the man, it was quietly shipped away to Churchill's country house. After his death, Mrs Churchill had it unceremoniously burnt.

Like Churchill, we all desire a glorious image. And we want others to see this. We want, so pitifully, to be portrayed gloriously—as spouses or parents or grandparents or workers or sports people or friends. We care deeply about the things people say about us behind our backs or on social media, as part of projecting this image of ourselves. Many of us have lived 'the miracle of the carpark'—the moment on a Sunday morning when we arrive at church to portray the image of a 'holy family' as we exit the car, even though we've been engaged in unholy bickering all the way to church.

8 'Sketch of a Scientist', *Distillations*, Spring 2018 (viewed 19 December 2018): www.sciencehistory.org/distillations/magazine/sketch-of-a-scientist.

9 '10 Controversial Portraits of Heads of State', *ListVerse*, 6 March 2018 (viewed 19 December 2018): www.listverse.com/2018/03/06/10-controversial-portraits-of-heads-of-state/

Just as the final portrait of Churchill fell far short of how he wished to be seen, so our true nature falls far short of what we wish we were. We fail to grasp the honour of being created in the image of God, of representing his office as his appointed rulers—not just of Great Britain, but of the whole world—under his loving lordship. We're image bearers, but we're fallen image bearers, failing to live as we ought and falling short of the glory of God (Rom 3:23).

But of course, where the rest of humanity fails so dismally, Jesus succeeds. Although fully human, Jesus is also the true image of the invisible God, representing the Father perfectly as the Ruler of the world. Out of his perfect love, the Father perfectly passes on his role to his Son. Whoever has seen the Son has seen the Father (John 14:9).

Like Father, like Son.

King of kings

The beloved Son is also described as "the firstborn of all creation". Clearly, this cannot mean that he is the first to be born among all *created* things, for Paul goes on to tell us explicitly that Jesus was *not* created. He is the agent of creation—with everything being created in him, through him, and for him.

Rather, the title of 'firstborn' has echoes of Jesus being the 'heir'—the one who stands to inherit all creation. Even more specifically, this is probably an allusion to Psalm 89:

He [King David] shall cry to me, "You are my Father,
    my God, and the Rock of my salvation."
And I will make him the firstborn,
    the highest of the kings of the earth. (Ps 89:26-27)

In other words, the 'firstborn' is 'the King of kings', the one who will rule on David's throne forever.

As you read through the Old Testament, you encounter many, many kings of Israel and Judah. A handful were good, though most would be best ranked somewhere between bad and disastrously bad. They were all 'firstborns', ruling on David's throne. They were all meant to be 'the King of kings', but even the best of them failed.

But not Jesus. He is the true 'firstborn', *the* King of kings.

Why is Jesus the true firstborn and the true King of kings? Again, the heart of the answer is found in verse 16: "For by him [or in him] all things were created, in heaven and on earth, visible and invisible, whether thrones or dominions or rulers or authorities—all things were created through him and for him".

God didn't create the world because he was lonely or because he needed somebody to love. God the Father, God the Son and God the Holy Spirit have been in perfect, loving relationship with each other since before time began. Every created thing—including you and me—is the overflow of God's love for his Son.

It is almost as if there is something gratuitous, something unnecessary, about creation. It is such an over-the-top expression of the Father's perfect love for his Son. When you stare at your favourite natural wonder, I hope you're filled with awe and joy in all kinds of ways, and I hope it drives you to remember the wonder of God's power and greatness. But above all, I hope you're reminded of the extraordinary love between God the Father and God the Son. For in the end, creation is anything but unnecessary. Everything visible, including you and me, was made for Jesus as an overflow of the Father's love for the Son.

'Spiritual warfare'

The New Testament makes very clear that the spiritual realm is real, and that God's people are engaged in a spiritual battle against Satan and his cohort, who seek to undermine our faith in Jesus and drag us away from obedience to him. In secularized parts of the world like most Western nations, it can be easy to forget that 'spiritual warfare' is part of the reality of our Christian lives. In other parts of the world, there is a heightened awareness of the spiritual realm—so much so that people can sometimes become overly fearful of Satan and his power.

We have to remember that Satan is real and is active in the world (e.g. 1 Pet 5:8), and yet that he has been defeated and stripped of his power in the death and resurrection of the Lord Jesus Christ (e.g. Col 2:15).

Which danger is bigger for you: the danger of ignoring Satan and his schemes, or the danger of becoming too fearful of Satan's power? What truths do you need to meditate on to help you find the right balance?

But Paul isn't only interested in the visible creation. He also says that everything *invisible* was made in, through and for Jesus. This includes the 'thrones', 'dominions', 'rulers' and 'authorities' mentioned in verse 16. When Paul uses this kind of language, he's referring to the spiritual realm, as in Ephesians 6:

> For we do not wrestle against flesh and blood, but against the rulers, against the authorities, against the cosmic powers over this present darkness, against the spiritual forces of evil in the heavenly places. (Eph 6:12)

'Rulers' and 'authorities' refer to invisible spiritual forces of evil—opposed to God, his purposes, and his people. There are evil spiritual forces at work in the heavenly places—but even they exist in Jesus, through Jesus, and for Jesus. They serve at the pleasure of King Jesus even as they rebel against him, for he sovereignly uses them for his good purposes.

Furthermore, as the Creator, the Son is "before all things" (1:17a). There was never a time when Jesus, the beloved and eternal Son of the Father, did not exist. And "in him all things hold together" (1:17b). Every atom, every molecule and every strand of DNA, not to mention every star and every galaxy, have Jesus to thank not only for their existence, but for their *ongoing* existence. Jesus sustains them all through every nanosecond of every day. Without his active sustaining power, creation would disintegrate. We would disintegrate.

Head of the church

In verse 18, Paul's focus shifts. So far, he's been considering Jesus' relationship to all of creation. Now, he narrows his focus: "And he is the head of the body, the church" (1:18a).

If Jesus is Lord of all things, and if he is supreme over all the forces of the universe, including the spiritual forces of evil, then why bother mentioning the church? It seems like such an anti-climax.

Today, many people in our secularized Western societies see the church as nothing more than a stuffy, outdated human institution—at best to be grudgingly tolerated, at worst to be opposed or preferably even eradicated. In a climate like that, it's easy to feel embarrassed about the 'church'.

But the church, rightly understood, is nothing to feel embarrassed about. For Jesus does not feel embarrassed about the church. He identifies himself very closely with his church. In fact, he is the head of the church. The 'church' that Paul has in mind is a people who will live on into the next age—unlike the creation, which will not continue (as it is) into the next age.

As well as the head of the church, Jesus is also "the beginning, the firstborn from the dead". In other words, he is not only the King of kings in this age; he is also the Ruler (the 'firstborn') of the age to come—an age where his saved people, the church, will also be present. In this sense, Jesus is 'preeminent' in 'everything'. He rules everything in this creation, and he rules everything in the age to come.

And why is Jesus preeminent in everything? "For in him all the fullness of God was pleased to dwell" (1:19). The baby born in a manger, the carpenter from Nazareth, the preacher who walked the streets of Galilee, who ate and slept, and went to the bathroom, and made friends and enemies—the one who was tried, convicted and nailed to a cross—this Jesus is God himself.

And as the one who was both fully God and fully man, Jesus was the only one who could accomplish the reconciliation of all things:

> For in him all the fullness of God was pleased to dwell,
> and through him to reconcile to himself all things,
> whether on earth or in heaven, making peace by the
> blood of his cross. (1:19-20)

As God, the beloved Son reconciles all things to himself. The "all things" mentioned here are the same "all things" covered back in verse 16—things visible and things invisible, including both the good and the evil spiritual forces. Jesus reconciles all things to himself by making peace between himself and his creation. This is a creation filled with 'darkness' (1:13), but which Jesus can still reconcile to himself by his bloody, violent death on the cross.

But how can "all things" truly be at peace with Jesus and reconciled to Jesus—either the rulers and authorities of the heavenly realms, or human beings living in the earthly realm? Other parts of Scripture teach us very clearly that not all people will ultimately be saved, so Paul's reference to "all things" cannot refer to some kind of universalism. Some have suggested that "all things" simply means something like "all *kinds of* things". This is an interesting suggestion, but ultimately unworkable. For it seems clear that Paul is at pains to show the *universal* nature of Jesus' authority. He does not just rule over all *kinds of* things; he rules over *all things*.

So what, then, does it mean when Paul says that Jesus reconciles "all things" to himself? We need to read the text very carefully at this point. After all, as someone told

> ### A text without a context is a con
>
> Words and phrases find their meaning in their context. There is the *literary* context (which identifies how the author links words, phrases, ideas and themes together) and the *historical* context (which explores the specific historical situation of the original readers). While the historical context can aid us greatly, our knowledge of it is always incomplete, and it should never overturn the plain meaning arising from the immediate literary context. Another crucial consideration is the *wider biblical* context: quotes from, or allusions to, the Old Testament or other parts of the New Testament, can be very important in determining the meaning of a word or phrase.

me many years ago, "a text without a context is a con". In particular, we need to pay careful attention to the immediate *literary* context, which trumps all other contexts. What does the text itself tell us?

In this context, reconciliation cannot refer *only* to enemies being made friends (even though that is generally what it means in the Bible). The scope of reconciliation here is something bigger and broader. In this context, where Paul is including the spiritual realm as well as the earthly realm, it most likely refers to bringing about *true and peaceful order in all creation.*

Think of an accountant 'reconciling' the books—bringing everything back into proper order. That's the kind of idea that Paul has in mind.

First and foremost, 'true and peaceful order' means receiving Christ Jesus as he is: as Lord. And within this true order, it's possible to receive Jesus *willingly* as Lord, or *unwillingly* as Lord. Every person will either enjoy reconciling *forgiveness* from Jesus or face reconciling *judgement* from Jesus. Both are, in one sense (i.e. in the sense of restoring true and peaceful order), reconciliation.

Look what happens for those who receive Jesus *willingly* as Lord:

> And you, who once were alienated and hostile in mind, doing evil deeds, he has now reconciled in his body of flesh by his death, in order to present you holy and blameless and above reproach before him... (1:21-22)

> And you, who were dead in your trespasses and the uncircumcision of your flesh, God made alive together

with him, having forgiven us all our trespasses, by canceling the record of debt that stood against us with its legal demands. This he set aside, nailing it to the cross. He disarmed the rulers and authorities and put them to open shame, by triumphing over them in him. (2:13-15)

All our deeds, all the sins for which we should have been punished, were kept on record as a debt. Without Jesus, things could only be brought into true order if we paid those debts ourselves. But thanks to Jesus, our debts are cancelled—because Jesus was punished "in his body of flesh" in your place and in mine when he died on the cross.

Pause and ponder this. Every fleshly act, every lustful thought, every impure motive, every lie, every slanderous word, every selfish act, every deed in my life that should provoke the wrath of God—all of it, every last bit, has now been cancelled. It's been set aside and nailed to the cross.

Do you know this to be true of yourself and of your own sin? I've learned over the years that it's entirely possible to spend lots of time around other Christians—to go to church regularly, to attend conferences, even to invest time in reading Christian books like this one—but to not actually know Jesus as Lord and Saviour.

This was my experience. In my first year as a university student, I attended a conference where the main speaker said, "If you want to know whether you are a Christian or not, ask yourself: is Jesus really number one in your life?" Although I was going to church regularly, reading Christian books and living a moral life, I realized Jesus still wasn't number one. He was a good number two or number three, someone I admired very much. But I knew Jesus wasn't number one. Only then did I turn to him as my Lord and Saviour.

So please take the time to answer these questions for yourself: Is Jesus really number one of your life? Have you come to know him as your Lord? Have you bowed the knee to him *willingly*? Do you enjoy his reconciling forgiveness?

Remember the fate of all those who do not willingly submit to his rule. Jesus has "disarmed the rulers and authorities and put them to open shame" in his death on the cross (2:15).[10] The same rulers and authorities who continue to war against Jesus in the invisible spiritual realm will also be reconciled to Jesus, but it will not be a reconciliation of forgiveness. Instead, it will be a reconciliation of judgement—of open shame, of sin being exposed and defeated—by the very same cross that brings the reconciliation of forgiveness.

Please be warned. It brings me no joy to write these words, but if you do not know Jesus as Lord, and if you have not willingly bowed the knee to him, then your 'deeds of the flesh' are still on your own record as a debt to be paid. You are facing the reconciling judgement of the Lord Jesus.

Whether you are young or old, a parent or a child, powerful or powerless, be warned. If you are a youth leader, Bible study leader or church pastor, be warned.

There is no refuge *from* Jesus. There is only refuge *in* Jesus.

But if you have received Christ Jesus as Lord, think again about the difference his reconciling forgiveness makes. We enjoy the refuge of being holy, blameless and above

---

10 The Greek word *autō* can be translated 'he' (i.e. Jesus; cf. ESV) or 'it' (i.e. the cross; cf. NIV). Based on the reference to the cross in 2:14, I believe it's most likely that Paul is referring to the cross at the end of 2:15.

reproach before Jesus, all because of his death for us. This is simply staggering!

And our perseverance in living for Jesus will serve as proof of this refuge. You will demonstrate you have been reconciled "if indeed you continue in the faith, stable and steadfast, not shifting from the hope of the gospel that you heard" (1:23a).

Many people today will suggest that it doesn't much matter what you believe, as long as you believe it sincerely. Nike, one of the world's biggest companies, ran a high-profile campaign based around the slogan "Believe in Something". But the Bible never tells us to "believe in something"; it tells us to "believe *in Jesus*". Paul does not speak of persevering in "*your* faith"; he speaks of persevering in "*the* faith".

"The faith" refers to a particular body of teaching, with the same expression being used in Colossians 2:7. It's clear from 1:23 that "*the* faith" is synonymous with "the gospel" (1:5). This 'gospel', this momentous news of Jesus, is the body of teaching that Epaphras first taught the Colossians. And continuing in this gospel will demonstrate that you take refuge in Jesus as Lord.

Paul also makes the bold claim that this same gospel has been "proclaimed in all creation under heaven" (1:23). This cannot mean that every single individual in the world has heard this news already. If the gospel has been proclaimed to literally every person under heaven, we wouldn't need any more missionaries. But Paul cannot mean this. Otherwise, he wouldn't have asked the Colossians to pray for his ongoing gospel proclamation (4:3-4).

So what does he mean in 1:23? Is he simply referring to Colossae and the surrounding cities as "the world" to which the gospel had already been proclaimed? That is, does he mean that the gospel has been proclaimed to every creature in the *known* world? This seems unlikely, given his universal language of "the whole world" back in 1:6, not to mention that he speaks of "all creation under heaven" in 1:23.

I suspect that Paul is addressing the nature of the gospel itself. He is describing the *kind* of gospel that he preaches. It is the "proclaimed in all creation under heaven" kind of gospel. This news of Jesus is so important, so momentous and so explosive, that it simply must be proclaimed in every last corner of the world. That is "the faith" we are called to continue in, and it's "the faith" that is for the whole world. If you come to see Christ and his gospel clearly, you can't help but long to see this gospel go out to the very ends of the earth.

Savour the fact that Jesus is God's beloved Son—in whom, through whom and for whom all things were made, because of God's overflowing love for his Son. Remind yourself over and over again that the real Jesus is the Creator and Sustainer of everything, visible and invisible, and that he is the head of the church. Build reminders into every routine that forms part of your life: every time you shave or drink your coffee or shower or get in the car or turn the light out at night, remind yourself that Jesus is actively sustaining you and the entire universe, and that he's in charge of it all.

And in whatever way you're able, proclaim the real Jesus to every tribe and people and nation. Proclaim that he is the one who reconciles all things to himself, whether willingly or unwillingly, by his death. Proclaim that he has been raised as the Ruler of this age and of the age to come. Proclaim that he is preeminent in everything and that he is the real King of kings, ruling over the seemingly powerful rulers of this world.

Jesus reigns and rules. No authority can ever rival him, because he is God's beloved Son.

Give thanks and pray

- Thank God for Jesus—especially that Jesus reigns and rules over the whole universe.
- Pray that God would help you to see and savour Jesus Christ as he truly is.
- Ask God to help you proclaim Jesus to the people around you and to the nations, so that many will come to know him and the reconciling forgiveness that he offers.

Discussion questions

- In what ways do we distort a clear view of who Jesus really is?
- What competes for our attention as we seek to see Jesus as he really is?
- How can we continue in "*the* faith" (the gospel)?

3 | Suffering in Christ

*H*e was brutally executed for high treason. After being arrested and tried, he was stripped naked, dragged through the streets, hung almost to the point of death, pulled from limb to limb, disemboweled and beheaded. His body was then quartered and sent to the four corners of England as a powerful warning. On 23 August 1305, William Wallace became a martyr in the fight for Scottish independence.

Everyone who has seen Wallace immortalized in Mel's Gibson's 1995 film *Braveheart* will remember the climactic moment—no doubt presented with a healthy dose of creative licence. As Wallace is about to die, he's given one last chance to plead for 'mercy' (in the form of a quick end to his suffering). But instead of crying out for mercy, he uses his last breath to triumphantly declare what he lived and died for: "FREEDOM!"

Wallace used many different tactics—raids on English outposts, guerilla warfare and even assassinations. But his strategy remained the same: to unite Scots in a willingness to suffer for their freedom. Wallace led the cause in his life and in his death. As has often been said, a person has only found something worth living for if they have found something worth dying for.

Rejoicing in suffering

The apostle Paul found something worth living and dying for. In fact, he went so far as to say he *rejoiced* in his suffering (Col 1:24). And he certainly had plenty of experience with suffering. Throughout his time as a Christian, he was frequently abused, beaten, persecuted and imprisoned. In 2 Corinthians 11:26, he says he was "in danger from rivers, danger from robbers, danger from my own people, danger from Gentiles, danger in the city, danger in the wilderness, danger at sea, danger from false brothers". I think it's safe to say he was in danger!

But why did he suffer? Was there any purpose to his sufferings? Was he just a masochist or was there a reason he could rejoice in his sufferings? What did he discover that was worth living for and dying for?

> Now I rejoice in my sufferings for your sake, and in my flesh I am filling up what is lacking in Christ's afflictions for the sake of his body, that is, the church, of which I became a minister according to the stewardship from God that was given to me for you... (1:24-25a)

Paul suffered for the sake of God's people—including the Colossian church that he had never even met face to face. Remember, Jesus is the head of this very church, and Paul understands that what happens to him in his flesh involves Jesus and Jesus' body, the church. Paul sees that his own sufferings are, in some way, "filling up what is lacking in Christ's afflictions".

What does this mean? It certainly doesn't mean that Paul thought he had to pay for his own sins. And it most emphatically doesn't mean Jesus' death was insufficient to pay for the sins of the Colossians, or indeed for the sins of the whole world. We know that beyond a shadow of a doubt based on what the rest of the New Testament teaches. For example, here's how the apostle Peter puts it: "Christ also suffered once for sins, the righteous for the unrighteous, that he might bring us to God" (1 Pet 3:18). And here's how Paul expressed it in his letter to the Corinthian church: "For our sake [God] made him to be sin who knew no sin, so that in him we might become the righteousness of God" (2 Cor 5:21). As theologian Roger Nicole wrote, "What Christ suffered is so immense, in fact so infinite, that it would be amply sufficient to atone for all the sins of all the people of all ages in the whole world and in a thousand worlds besides, if these existed".[11]

So in what sense can Jesus' sufferings or afflictions be at all *lacking*? How is it that they need to be "filled up"?

Let's begin to answer those questions by delving back into Paul's past. You might remember that, before he was known as Paul, he was known as Saul. Before his conversion to be a follower of Christ, Saul was a virulent enemy of Christ. In fact, he devoted himself to persecuting Christians:

11 Roger Nicole, *Our Sovereign Saviour: The Essence of the Reformed Faith*, Christian Focus, Ross-shire, Scotland, 2002, p. 58.

Saul, still breathing threats and murder against the disciples of the Lord, went to the high priest and asked him for letters to the synagogues at Damascus, so that if he found any belonging to the Way, men or women, he might bring them bound to Jerusalem. Now as he went on his way, he approached Damascus, and suddenly a light from heaven shone around him. And falling to the ground, he heard a voice saying to him, "Saul, Saul, why are you persecuting me?" And he said, "Who are you, Lord?" And he said, "I am Jesus, whom you are persecuting." (Acts 9:1-5)

On the surface of it, Saul hadn't been persecuting *Jesus*. He was persecuting *Christians*. Jesus had risen from the dead and ascended to be with his Father in heaven. And yet Jesus so identifies himself with his people that to persecute his people *is* to persecute Jesus. To cause the church to suffer *is* to cause Jesus to suffer.

So, what is lacking in Christ's afflictions? **The afflictions of persecution that all Christians will face, to some degree, until Jesus returns**.

History bears witness to this reality. In the first century, Christians suffered greatly under Imperial Rome. In the fourth century, a great persecution broke out under the Emperor Diocletian, forcing Christians to comply with Rome's pagan religion. Persecution intensified again in the Middle Ages. During the Reformation, reformer after reformer was burnt at the stake.

In 2018, over 245 million Christians faced intimidation, prison, or even death for their faith in Jesus. One in nine

Christians worldwide were persecuted for their faith.[12] Every year, Open Doors publishes its 'World Watch List'—a catalogue of "the 50 most dangerous countries to follow Jesus". It makes for sobering reading. In 2019, the top ten countries are North Korea, Afghanistan, Somalia, Libya, Pakistan, Sudan, Eritrea, Yemen, Iran and India.[13] As Christians all over the world face suffering and persecution, Jesus suffers too. What is 'lacking' is not the atoning sacrifice of Jesus, but the ongoing suffering of his people that must and will continue until Jesus returns.

In Revelation 6:10, those who have been martyred for Jesus cry out, "O Sovereign Lord, holy and true, how long before you will judge and avenge our blood on those who dwell on the earth?" It's a question that echoes down through the ages: How long, O Lord? The answer comes in verse 11: "until the number of their fellow servants and their brothers should be complete, who were to be killed as they themselves had been".

In other words, Jesus will not return until the appropriate number of martyrs has been reached. In Colossian terms, what is 'lacking' is a sufficient and complete number of martyrs.

I suspect that most of us living in the West will not be called upon to die for Jesus—at least not any time soon—though being forced to go to prison is not beyond the realm of possibility. We don't know the details of what the future

---

12 'About Persecution', *Open Doors Australia*, 2019 (viewed 29 January 2019): www.opendoors.org.au/persecuted-christians/about-persecution/.

13 'World Watch List: The 50 most dangerous countries to follow Jesus', *Open Doors Australia*, 2019 (viewed 29 January 2019): www.opendoors.org.au/persecuted-christians/world-watch-list/.

holds, but we know it will involve suffering. Did not Jesus say, "If anyone would come after me, let him deny himself and take up his cross and follow me" (Mark 8:34)? As Don Carson has said, we must live as if it is better to die than to be faithless.[14] It is better to die than to lie, gossip, steal or commit sexual immorality. It is better to die than to be ashamed of Christ in the face of strident secularism. To be a follower of Jesus will inevitably involve suffering.

Paul experienced his particular share of this suffering, as Jesus' appointed apostle to the nations:

> But the Lord said to [Ananias], "Go, for [Saul] is a chosen instrument of mine to carry my name before the Gentiles and kings and the children of Israel. For I will show him how much he must suffer for the sake of my name." (Acts 9:15-16)

Paul wasn't just Jesus' instrument to preach the gospel for the sake of his name; he was also Jesus' instrument to *suffer* for the sake of his name. He filled up in his flesh his share of what was still lacking in Christ's afflictions, as the unique, joyful, suffering apostle to the nations. His suffering did not bring about the Colossians' salvation, but as John Stott so eloquently put it, Paul's suffering was "an indispensable link in the chain of their salvation".[15]

But even as Paul suffered in this way, his driving concern was to preach the gospel of Jesus:

---

14 DA Carson, *How Long, O Lord? Reflections on Suffering and Evil,* Baker, Grand Rapids, MI, 1990, p. 120.

15 John Stott, *The Cross of Christ,* IVP, Leicester, 1998, p. 322.

...I became a minister according to the stewardship from God that was given to me for you, to make the word of God fully known, the mystery hidden for ages and generations but now revealed to his saints. (1:25b-26)

When Paul speaks of a 'mystery', he is not referring to something that remains hidden and can never be fully uncovered. Nor is it a mystery in the sense of being 'weird' or 'spooky'. Rather, he is speaking of something that remained concealed for a time but has now been revealed.

Remember, as we saw in chapter 1, that at this point Paul is using the word 'saints' to refer specifically to Jewish Christians. So what has now been revealed to Jewish Christians, at this key moment in salvation history, is that Gentiles too can have Christ dwell in them: "To them [Jewish Christians] God chose to make known how great among the Gentiles are the riches of the glory of this mystery, which is Christ in you, the hope of glory" (1:27).

This is a mystery with eternal significance—something that was always there to be understood based on the Old Testament prophets, but which not even the prophets themselves fully understood at the time. The mystery remained hidden for "ages and generations", and was only revealed with the coming of Christ.

It's hard to overstate how earth-shattering this change was for those in the Jewish community in Jesus' day. They had come to think of Gentiles as being synonymous with prostitutes, tax collectors and sinners. But now, Paul says that these very same Gentiles can stand before God on equal footing with the 'saints'. They receive the same promises and the same blessings. They look forward to the same inheritance.

Here is the 'mystery' of Paul's gospel: Jesus is for all the nations, Jewish and Gentile alike. Jesus is the international Christ. He is the Lord of all.

Everyone mature in Christ

This is the ultimate "hope of glory" shared by all those who have faith in Jesus. That's why we read these great words in Colossians 1:28—words that capture the heart and the essence of Paul's ministry: "Him we proclaim, warning everyone and teaching everyone with all wisdom, that we may present everyone mature in Christ".

Look back at that verse and take note of the word Paul repeats three times: *everyone*. We warn *everyone*. We teach *everyone*. We long to present *everyone* mature in Christ. This gospel is for every person in the whole world. As Paul says later in Colossians, "Here there is not Greek and Jew, circumcised and uncircumcised, barbarian, Scythian, slave, free; but Christ is all, and in

A perfect verse to keep us focused

The Australian Fellowship of Evangelical Students (AFES) has long used Colossians 1:28 as the basis for its mission statement: "Proclaiming Jesus Christ at university to present everyone mature in him". It's a verse that can keep any church and any Christian ministry moving in the right direction: proclaim Christ, with the goal of presenting everyone mature in him. It's also a verse that can keep any Christian personally focused in life and ministry: To whom am I proclaiming Christ? What am I doing to help achieve the goal of presenting *everyone* mature in him?

all" (3:11). That's why he proclaims Christ with unending passion and determination.

This is the essence of the Christian message. This is what we hope and pray that missionaries around the globe will continue to do—whether in the affluent, Christianized West or in gospel-poor parts of the world. This is the heart of what Christians must proclaim in public and in private, in the marketplace and in the home, in the writing of letters and the sending of emails, or even if we stand before governors and courts. We proclaim Christ. We proclaim Christ to *everyone*.

But the faithful preacher of Christ must do this courageously. It takes God-given boldness to persevere toward the goal of presenting everyone mature in him. Truth matters, and if we're going to proclaim Christ then we'll need to contend for the truth and, indeed, suffer for the truth.

Furthermore, proclaiming Christ will involve teaching everyone *with all wisdom.*

On the one hand, Christ himself *is* the embodiment of wisdom—the one "in whom are hidden all the treasures of wisdom and knowledge" (2:3). So when we proclaim Christ, the very content of our message will be the epitome of wisdom.

On the other hand, it will take wisdom from above to know how Christ should be most clearly and faithfully proclaimed in different languages and cultures. For example, it will take God's wisdom to figure out what restrictions or laws of the land we can comply with, and what we could never agree to or compromise on in order to stay faithful to Christ and his gospel.

But whatever the culture, whatever the restrictions or

barriers placed before us, we proclaim Christ. We proclaim the beloved Son of the Father—in whom, through whom and for whom all things were created. We proclaim the head of the church. We proclaim the one who reconciles all things to himself through his death and resurrection. We proclaim the one who is Lord of all.

Proclaiming Christ is hard work. It will take an enormous amount of energy. But *whose* energy?

Toiling with his energy

Paul toils and struggles to the point of exhaustion so that he can proclaim this gospel, but he doesn't do this in his own strength: "For this I toil, struggling with all his energy that he powerfully works within me" (1:29). The word translated 'struggling' is the Greek word *agonizomai*, which is, as you can probably tell, the word from which we get the English word 'agonize'. But this agonizing struggle isn't possible because Paul digs deep into his own heart, his own strength or his own resources. It's possible because he relies on Christ's energy being at work in him.

Does this mean we 'let go and let God' or that there's no need for us to work hard in ministry? Not at all. Paul is still able to say, "For this *I* toil". The man worked hard and gave his all to make Jesus known. Yet he knew that undergirding all his toil was the powerful work of God enabling him to engage in the struggle.

In other words, we can only proclaim Christ because Christ himself gives us the energy and the ability to do so. The successful proclamation of Christ does not ultimately depend on us and on our agonizing ministry, but on Christ being at work in and through our ministry.

This is why, at the beginning of chapter 2, Paul makes the Colossians aware of his struggles: "For I want you to know how great a struggle I have for you and for those at Laodicea and for all who have not seen me face to face...". I have to admit, this verse used to confuse me. Why does he need us to know about his struggle? Is it just to have his ego massaged or to win our admiration or sympathy? "Oh, poor Paul, he's given up *so* much and he's working *so* hard! What a guy!"

If you ask your pastor how things are going in life and ministry, it's unlikely that he'll say, "You know what? I am completely living the dream!" Christian ministry is a long, hard slog. Yet occasionally pastors and gospel workers can face the temptation to focus on their hardships so that you'll admire them even more.

But not Paul. He doesn't share his struggles so that they can focus on *his* efforts, but so that they can focus on *Christ's* efforts. He wants the Colossians to understand his struggle so that they will come to see that *God* is at work. Christ's purpose is to present everyone mature in himself. He does that through weak, frail servants like Paul, like me and like you. And it happens this way so that Jesus alone will get the glory.

Here, then, is God's infallible strategy to reach the nations with the gospel of Jesus—to have a world that knows Jesus: **the prayerful proclamation of Jesus to all the nations through suffering**.

Our *tactics* may differ from ministry to ministry or from church to church, and our tactics are fallible and changeable. For example, you may have heard of the 'five Ms' model of church life.[16] Some churches are committed to this model, while others are not. We may embrace particular evangelistic courses, such as 'Christianity Explored' or 'Two Ways to Live', or we may opt for a less structured approach to evangelism. We may have highly organized welcoming teams or a more informal method. You may organize Bible study groups corporately in the church building or separately in people's homes. All those *tactical* decisions are open to change and contextually fallible.

However, our God-given *strategy* is infallible, precisely because it is *God-given*. It will never fail. And God's strategy is the prayerful proclamation of Jesus to all the nations through suffering.[17]

This is why Paul willingly embraces suffering:

> ...that their [i.e. all who haven't seen him face to face] hearts may be encouraged, being knit together in love, to reach all the riches of full assurance of understanding and the knowledge of God's mystery, which is Christ, in whom are hidden all the treasures of wisdom and knowledge. (2:2-3)

Once again, Paul wants the Colossians' focus to be on Jesus, not him. He aims to present them mature in Christ and this maturity involves both a supernatural love for one another

---

16 The 'five Ms' is an approach in which churches organize their ministry and staff teams around five purposes: Magnification, Ministry, Maturity, Membership and Mission.

17 I am indebted to Phillip Jensen for his insights on the difference between 'tactics' and 'strategy'. For more, see 'The Strategy of God', *PhillipJensen.com*, 26 November 2009 (viewed 18 December 2018): www.phillipjensen.com/the-strategy-of-god/.

and a crystal-clear vision of the person and work of Jesus. Christian maturity involves recognizing that *all* the treasures of wisdom and knowledge are found not at Oxford or Harvard, or in the media, or in the opinion polls, or whomever the latest guru is this week. Nor are all the treasures of wisdom and knowledge found in your favourite Christian website, your favourite celebrity pastor and definitely not in the author of this book! All the treasures of wisdom and knowledge are found *solely* in Jesus Christ.

And Paul understands that getting this right is a matter of urgency: "I say this in order that no-one may delude you with plausible arguments" (2:4). That's why part of proclaiming Christ will, from time to time, involve refuting false teaching and exposing false arguments. To look for ultimate wisdom outside of Jesus is dangerous and delusional. I'll say more about this in the next chapter.

Once you start to see Christ clearly,[18] it will fuel you to persevere in godliness and in gospel ministry. Paul rejoiced that he had heard about the Colossians showing this kind of perseverance: "For though I am absent in body, yet I am with you in spirit, rejoicing to see your good order and the firmness of your faith in

> **All wisdom and knowledge**
>
> Which source of 'wisdom' are you most tempted to trust over and above Jesus Christ? Is it, for example, a pastor, an author, a speaker, an institution or a website? Do you ever find it difficult to believe that "all the treasures of wisdom and knowledge" are hidden in Christ? Spend some time asking God to help you see this clearly.

---

18 And if you're struggling with this, can I suggest you read Colossians 1:15-20 again?

Christ" (2:5). We should rejoice every time we hear of someone putting their faith in Jesus for the first time and we should rejoice when we hear of Jesus' servants persevering and bearing fruit.

When we hear of God's people persevering, it should make our hearts sing, for this is the fruit of God's powerful energy at work in his suffering, agonized servants that he has sent throughout the world. Indeed, this is how Paul sees himself: as a 'minister' (or, more accurately, a 'servant') of the gospel (1:23) and a 'minister' (or 'servant') of the church (1:24-25). To be a servant of the church is to be a servant of the gospel. And to be a servant of the gospel is to suffer. Look at how John Stott captured these ideas:

> The place of suffering in service and of passion in mission is hardly ever taught today. But **the greatest single secret of evangelistic or missionary effectiveness is a willingness to suffer and die.** It may be a death to popularity (by faithfully preaching the unpopular biblical gospel), or to pride (by the use of modest methods in reliance on the Holy Spirit), or to racial and national prejudice (by identification with another culture), or to material comfort (by adopting a particular lifestyle). But the servant must suffer if he is to bring light to the nations, and the seed must die if it is to multiply.[19]

This is simply staggering. Are we truly willing to suffer and die for Jesus? Are we truly willing to be unpopular, to humble ourselves, to cross cultural boundaries and to give up our material comforts in order to proclaim Christ? Only

19 Stott, *The Cross of Christ*, p. 313 (emphasis mine).

when we can answer yes to those questions have we truly embraced the strategy of God: the prayerful proclamation of Jesus to all the nations *through suffering.*

Richard Johnson was the first chaplain to Australia, arriving with the First Fleet in 1788. Johnson's 'spiritual father' was John Newton, who's probably best-known as the author of the hymn 'Amazing Grace'. But Newton was also one of the great pastoral letter writers in the history of the church.[20]

At one point, Johnson wrote Newton a letter regarding how deeply discouraged he felt about his ministry in the fledgling colony of Sydney. In his reply, Newton wrote these incredible words:

> I have not been disheartened by your apparent want of success. I have been told that skilful gardeners will undertake to sow and raise a salad for dinner in the short time while the meat is roasting. But no gardener can raise oaks with such expedition. You are sent to New Holland, not to sow salad seeds, but to plant acorns; and your labour will not be lost, though the first appearances may be very small, and the progress very slow. You are, I trust, planting for the next century. I have a good hope that your oaks will one day spring up and flourish, and produce other acorns, which, in due time, will take root, and spread among the islands and nations in the Southern Ocean.[21]

20 For more on Newton's life and ministry, especially his extraordinary ministry of pastoral letter-writing, see Tony Reinke, *Newton on the Christian Life: To Live is Christ,* Crossway, Wheaton, IL, 2015.

21 See Craig Schwarze, 'John Newton: Australia's Godfather', *Sydney Anglicans.net,* 31 August 2010 (viewed 19 December 2018): www.sydney-anglicans.net/blogs/australias_godfather.

My home is in Australia—part of the 'Southern Ocean'. And I can testify that, by God's grace, Newton's hopes have been wonderfully fulfilled. Throughout this region, countless 'gospel acorns' have been planted and have grown. Thousands of churches and gospel ministries have taken root and in God's kindness our region has started to send many, many missionaries all over the world.

In the providence of God, this started with Richard Johnson—who, thanks to the encouragement of his friend John Newton, was willing to suffer and endure hardship for the sake of the Lord Jesus Christ. Here was a man who understood the strategy of God: **the prayerful proclamation of Jesus to all the nations *through suffering*.**

Are you willing to suffer for the gospel?

For if you are not willing to suffer for the gospel, you are not worthy to be a minister of the gospel.

But if you are willing to suffer, then—and only then—have you understood why Paul could rejoice in his sufferings. This is not masochism. This is joy in the infallible strategy of God—joy that embraces the growth of the gospel in our lives and in all the world, whatever the cost.

Give thanks and pray

- Thank God for sending Jesus to suffer for us and die the death that we deserved.
- Thank God for Paul and for other servants of Jesus who have suffered for Jesus' sake.
- Pray that God would help you to joyfully embrace his infallible strategy: the prayerful proclamation of Jesus to all the nations through suffering.

- Pray that God would give you a willingness to suffer for the sake of the gospel.

Discussion questions

- What does it mean for Paul to fill up in his flesh "what is lacking in Christ's afflictions"?
- What suffering are you anticipating in your context for proclaiming Christ?
- How can we toil with Christ's energy to endure this suffering?

4 | Walking in Christ

*B*efore he became a Christian, John Wesley went to the mission field and sought to 'convert' Native Americans. By his own admission, it wasn't until four months after this missionary trip that Wesley understood the gospel and was saved. God would later use him to bring revival to England through his powerful gospel preaching.

However, as a conservative high churchman, Wesley saw the idea of outdoor preaching as 'vile'. But his friend George Whitefield persuaded him that it was a good and worthwhile pursuit. Concerning his first outdoor sermon, Wesley wrote:

> At four in the afternoon, I submitted to be more 'vile', and proclaimed in the highways the glad tidings of salvation, speaking from a little eminence in a ground adjoining to the city, to about three thousand people.[22]

22 From Wesley's journal, 2 April 1739. Quoted in 'Four John Wesley quotes everyone should know', *JamesPedlar.wordpress*, 21 May 2011 (viewed 19 December 2018): www.jamespedlar.wordpress.com/2011/05/21/four-john-wesley-quotes-everyone-should-know/.

Two months later, Wesley famously wrote, "I look upon all the world as my parish".[23] He had rightly come to recognize that the gospel of Christ is for the whole world.

I wonder whether he had been reflecting on Paul's words in Colossians 1:28: "Him we proclaim, warning *everyone* and teaching *everyone* with all wisdom, that we may present *everyone* mature in Christ". Our apostle saw the whole world as his mission field, because the gospel is for the whole world.

Remember God's infallible strategy for the salvation of the world: **the prayerful proclamation of Jesus to all the nations through suffering**. And remember Paul's goal through his suffering: to present everyone *mature* in Christ.

Since maturity is the goal for quite literally everyone, we have to ask: what does it look like? This question brings us to perhaps the key verses of the entire letter—what some commentators have called "the heart of the letter"[24] or "the hinge around which the book turns":[25]

Therefore, as you received Christ Jesus the Lord, so walk in him, rooted and built up in him and established in the faith, just as you were taught, abounding in thanksgiving. (2:6-7)

---

23 Wesley's journal, 11 June 1739, quoted in 'Four John Wesley quotes everyone should know'.
24 Peter T O'Brien, *Colossians-Philemon*, Word Biblical Commentary, Thomas Nelson, Colombia, SC, 1982, p. 104.
25 Phillip D Jensen and Tony Payne, *Colossians: The Complete Christian*, Interactive Bible Studies, Matthias Media, Sydney, 2010, p. 7.

Receive and walk

Let's note the two key ideas. First, we are to *receive* Christ Jesus as Lord. This means recognizing Jesus for who he really is. It means living for him as the beloved Son—the one in whom, through whom and for whom all things were made. It means living for him as the head of the church and trusting him as the one who reconciles all things to himself. It means living for him as the one who is preeminent—the one who is Lord of all, the international Christ. This is the one we are to *receive*.

Second, we are to *walk* in him. Your 'walk' refers to your way of life. And we are to 'walk' in Jesus in the same way that we received him: as Lord. We are not to walk away from him or apart from him. We are not even to walk with him. We are walk *in him*, because he already dwells in us. Paul says that we must be "rooted and built up *in him*", for this is how we are "established in the faith".

On a narrow strip of land in northern California, just along the coastline, grow the giant Redwood trees. They are the biggest living things on earth. Some are over 100 metres tall or around the height of a 30-storey building. The roots that are needed to support these trees extend up to 30 metres away from the trunk.

Just like a mighty Redwood, we mature in Christ by being firmly "rooted" in him.

Or think of a building like the 30-storey hotel in China that was built to withstand a magnitude-9 earthquake. Such a building can only survive with the strongest possible foundations. And we can only survive in the Christian life, and we can only mature in the Christian life, if we are "built up" in Christ with the strongest possible foundations.

Walking in Christ will also involve being "established in the faith". Remember what we saw back in 1:23: Paul doesn't urge each of us to be established in "*your* faith", but in "*the* faith", the body of teaching that is the gospel. We should saturate ourselves in the explosive good news of Jesus.

And all this will involve "abounding in thanksgiving". One very clear sign of a Christian who's growing in their maturity is their thankfulness. If you're a complainer or you have an anger problem, could this be a sign that you really have a thankfulness problem? Mature Christians have a gospel-saturated thankfulness.

Do you know anyone like this? Do you know a Christian who just exudes this sense of thankfulness, even in hard times? Don't you find that person so encouraging? Wouldn't you love to be that kind of person for someone else?

I think of a wonderful couple named Dudley and Elizabeth Foord. Dudley passed away in 2013 at age 90, but he lived a life filled with joy and thankfulness. Dudley was a great Christian leader and was known for many things, but perhaps he's best known for wearing a broad grin and pumping his fist in the air in triumph and thankfulness as he remembered his Lord and Saviour.

Elizabeth is no less extraordinary a saint. When I had the chance to talk with her, I asked her how she avoided feeling resentful when she was at home with small children while her husband travelled the world speaking at conferences and Christian events. She replied, "I was always grateful that he could be there proclaiming Christ. It was hard work being on my own with the children, but I was always filled with thanks to God."

That's the kind of Christian maturity that Paul has in mind here—walking so closely in Christ, so rooted and established in him, that thankfulness simply overflows.

Don't be deceived

Sadly, there are many dangerous distractions that can stifle our walk in Christ—distractions that threaten to move us away from the way in which we received him. That's why, as we proclaim Christ and as we seek to walk in him for ourselves, it will involve "*warning* everyone and *teaching* everyone with all wisdom" (1:28). And that's why, after the positive words of 2:6-7, Paul provides the negative side of the coin:

> See to it that no-one takes you captive by philosophy and empty deceit, according to human tradition, according to the elemental spirits of the world, and not according to Christ. (2:8)

This doesn't refer to the study of philosophy *per se*. Philosophy is literally a 'love of wisdom' and it is simply the study of how people think and why they think in these ways. Thinking about how people think is a good and helpful thing to do. In fact, I'd argue that it's an essential part of theological thinking and effective gospel proclamation.

What Paul has in mind is to ensure we are not being *captured* by wrong thinking. So he warns Christians that they must not be captured by lies or by what other people say, rather than by what Christ says. He warns us not to be captured by deceitful world views that arise out of wrong philosophical thinking. It's good to understand how other people think and it's good to analyze the foundations of our own thinking. But if we're persuaded by wrong or deceitful philosophies, then we've been captured.

This is what Paul means by "the elemental spirits of the world". A more accurate translation of this phrase would be "the basic principles of the world" or perhaps even simply "the *elements* of the world". Paul is speaking of the most basic units of 'the world', which, for the Greeks, were the basic elements of earth, wind, fire and water. It's his metaphorical way of describing the basic philosophies of this dark world, which are based on lies.

Lies have their foundation in Satan. After all, Jesus himself calls Satan "the father of lies" (John 8:44). He is "the spirit that is now at work in the sons of disobedience" (Eph 2:2). As such, lies are simply forms of worldly "human tradition". This might include ideas and philosophies that are ever so attractive and impressive, seemingly wise in the eyes of our friends and neighbours. But if they are not based on Christ—or if they take us away from Christ and give us a distorted view of Christ—then they are destructive.

Let me offer a contemporary example. In his bestselling book *Good to Great*, Jim Collins shows companies how to change their culture and achieve "enduring greatness".[26] By God's common grace, this book contains plenty of helpful wisdom and we may even use some of these ideas to glorify God in our churches and ministries. For example, one of Collins's key points is that the best companies have humble CEOs. As followers of the 'Servant King', Christians can't help but agree with that observation.

---

26 Jim Collins, *Good to Great: Why Some Companies Make the Leap and Others Don't*, HarperCollins, New York, 2001, p. 20.

However, be careful. Don't be captured by the book's underlying world view. For the irony of Collins's system is that the whole reason to be humble is so that you can ultimately become *great*. In the end, this is still a pursuit of personal, worldly greatness.

Remember James and John, the "Sons of Thunder"? These are the men who came to Jesus, as recorded in Mark 10 and asked for the seats of glory—one at his right hand and one at his left hand. Even if we give them credit for their boldness, it's an ugly request. They desired personal, worldly greatness. At that time, they hadn't understood the first thing about Jesus or about following him. So Jesus rebuked them:

> "You know that those who are considered rulers of the Gentiles lord it over them, and their great ones exercise authority over them. But it shall not be so among you. But whoever would be great among you must be your servant, and whoever would be first among you must be slave of all. For even the Son of Man came not to be served but to serve, and to give his life as a ransom for many." (Mark 10:42-45)

Don't be captured by the 'elements' of this dark world, or by anything that leads us away from Jesus.

Defence against the dark arts

I'm told that experts in identifying counterfeit money do their job by getting to know authentic currency very, very well. The better you know the real thing, the better you'll be able to detect a fake.

Similarly, the first and best defence against the 'elements of the world' is to get to know Christ deeply. When Paul begins verse 9 with the crucial word 'for', it connects the warning of verse 8 with everything that follows, right up to and including verse 15.

So what do we see when we see Jesus clearly? Put simply, we see God:

> For in him the whole fullness of deity dwells bodily, and you have been filled in him, who is the head of all rule and authority. (2:9-10)

The best defence against the dark arts (with apologies to Harry Potter fans) is to see Jesus clearly as fully God. There is no more deity elsewhere.[27] You cannot get more of God than you get with Jesus. Indeed, as we've seen, God was pleased to have all his fullness dwell in Jesus (1:19).

And somehow, if Jesus is our Lord, then we have been "filled in him". The idea of being "filled" in Jesus is not about Jesus physically indwelling us—as though he fills up the gaps between our organs or anything like that. Rather, this is about our *spiritual* union with Christ. And Paul now unpacks the idea by turning to the concepts of circumcision and baptism:

> In him also you were circumcised with a circumcision made without hands, by putting off the body of the flesh, by the circumcision of Christ, having been buried with him in baptism, in which you were also

---

27 cf. John Woodhouse, *Colossians & Philemon: So Walk in Him*, Focus on the Bible, Christian Focus, Ross-shire, Scotland, 2011, p. 129.

raised with him through faith in the powerful working of God, who raised him from the dead. (2:11-12)

Remember, Paul is speaking to Gentile Christians who were not physically circumcised.[28] So when he says, "In him *also* you were circumcised", the point is that "even *you Gentiles*" were metaphorically 'circumcised' when you turned to Jesus. This is not a physical circumcision done with hands, but a spiritual reality that Jesus himself brings about. And the circumcision of Christ involves "putting off the body of the flesh".

Both these ideas—circumcision and putting off the body of the flesh—are probably vivid ways of referring to the death of Jesus. Instead of stripping off a small piece of flesh in physical circumcision, in Christ we have had our "body of the flesh", our sins, removed through the death of Jesus.[29] We are so deeply connected to Jesus and his death that we have been "buried with him" in baptism. We are fully immersed, not in water, but in his death for our sins—so much so that, when Jesus died, we died with him. And not only that, but we have also been raised with Jesus.

To be "filled" in Christ, then, is **to have all the benefits of Christ's life, death and resurrection because we are united with him**.

Furthermore, as we saw in 2:13-15 (back in chapter 2 of this book), we have had all our sins forgiven. Every sinful act, every deed in my life that would have rightly provoked

28 Circumcision was a sign of the covenant that God made with his people, the nation of Israel, in the Old Testament (first given to Abraham in Genesis 17). All Jewish males were to be circumcised at eight days of age as a sign that they belonged to the covenant people of God.

29 cf. O'Brien, *Colossians-Philemon*, p. 117.

the wrath of God, has now been set aside and nailed to the cross. And every demonic force has been disarmed through that same cross.

Why would anyone turn to the 'elements' of the world? For how can we surpass being in Christ? How can the world offer anything that exceeds dying with Christ and being raised with Christ? We cannot experience Christ more fully and we cannot outstrip being in Christ—because all of God's fullness dwells in him. And we have been filled in Christ. Why would you embrace any world view that leaves this Jesus out of the picture?

Captured by shadows

Do you see how knowing Christ, and knowing our union with Christ, helps us to discern error and to avoid being taken captive by deceitful philosophies? Once we have this discernment, we can avoid being captured by shadows:

> Therefore let no-one pass judgement on you in questions of food and drink, or with regard to a festival or a new moon or a Sabbath. These are a shadow of the things to come, but the substance belongs to Christ. (2:16-17)

What's wrong with the Sabbath? What's wrong with various Old Testament festivals? Nothing. At least nothing in and of themselves. God himself instituted all these positive rituals to which the prophet Ezekiel refers (cf. Ezek 45:17) and Paul isn't denigrating them.

But even though God himself instituted and commanded these rituals as part of the old covenant, and even though they were part of his revealed will for his people, they were only ever *shadows* of the reality. And the reality has now come: Jesus Christ, the one in whom all the fullness of the deity dwells. All the good and righteous laws and rituals that God established were only ever pointing to Jesus. To relate to God through the old covenant laws today is like ignoring your friend and relating only to their shadow.

Even under the old covenant, these good and holy laws still justly condemned us. But remember, Jesus has succeeded where Israel failed. He not only fulfilled the law, but he also cancelled its debt of condemnation by taking this condemnation upon himself in his death on the cross. What a spectacular distraction it would be, then, to return to the laws of the old covenant. What a deceitful distraction it would be to slide back into the shadows instead of coming into Christ's marvelous light.

Some friends of mine serve in student ministry in a Pacific nation. They recently shared their grief at seeing Christian students taken away from Jesus by a virulent strain of Seventh Day Adventist theology. They wrote in a prayer newsletter, "It is being strongly pushed that going to church on Saturday and not eating certain foods are essential to salvation". And my friends grieved at seeing many students deceived by mere shadows.

What a tragedy when real lives are destroyed by false teaching and by the distractions of this dark world. Don't allow yourself to be captured by mere shadows that point to Christ.

False disqualifications

At the same time, don't allow yourself to be captured by false disqualifications:

> Let no-one disqualify you, insisting on asceticism and worship of angels, going on in detail about visions, puffed up without reason by his sensuous mind, and not holding fast to the Head, from whom the whole body, nourished and knit together through its joints and ligaments, grows with a growth that is from God. (2:18-19)

Here are people who suggest that Jesus is not enough—that you need to have other supernatural experiences like visions or encounters with angels or ascetic commitments where you deny yourself bodily pleasures. But these people are disconnected from Jesus, the Head, as they seek to worship angels or pursue other experiences.

In this context, why mention angels? In Acts 7:53 and Galatians 3:19, we learn that angels were given the task of putting God's laws into effect. Indeed, angels were present when God gave Moses the Ten Commandments (cf. Acts 7:38). Therefore, it seems likely that some among the Colossians were dangerously distracted by angels, thinking they could potentially provide experiences that exceeded Christ or were missing in Christ.

What about asceticism? This

Spiritual experiences

Have you or your friends encountered the idea that certain 'spiritual experiences' are essential to salvation? What form do these 'experiences' take? How does Paul's teaching in Colossians equip you to respond to these ideas?

involves denying yourself physical pleasures such as food, drink or sex. Asceticism arose from a low view of the body, which in turn came out of the Greek philosophical approach that saw the soul as the 'real you', with the body merely discarded at death before the soul moved onto the spiritual realm. In this world view, salvation is all about freeing the soul from the body that dragged it down.

Asceticism has taken many different forms down through the centuries. In the 18th century, brothers John and Charles Wesley founded what mockingly became known as the 'Holy Club'. Members of the Holy Club fasted until 3pm on Wednesdays and Fridays, received Holy Communion once a week, discussed the Greek New Testament and various classic writings each evening and visited prisoners and the sick. They systematically brought every part of their lives under strict review.

Disciplines like these are not wrong in themselves. But what value do they have when they are detached from the gospel of Christ? John Wesley himself later confessed that he was not a Christian at the time he was part of the Holy Club. His discipline became a form of inadvertent asceticism as he tried to get closer to God without actually being converted.

In many ways, asceticism may not be the most dangerous distraction that we face as Western Christians today. Perhaps a handful of us may walk a fine line with disciplines like, 'No Bible, no breakfast'. But for the most part, it's not the greatest threat to our discipleship.

However, the deceitful world view behind asceticism is certainly a danger. Because the idea behind this form of asceticism is that freedom in Christ is all about giving prominence or expression to your 'inner self'—your *true* self, or the equivalent of your soul. It's about making sure that the soul escapes the constraints of the body in order to find one's 'true self'. A Christianized form of ascetic philosophy, then, culminates in the attitude that what pleases God is to be authentic to this 'true self', which is a 'self' detached from the constraints of the body.

Stop and ponder for a moment: isn't this a big part of what drives the LGBTQ community today? Increasingly, in this world view, the body is to be conformed to the 'true self', rather than the sense of 'true self' being conformed to the body.

But please remember what Jesus says about your 'true self':

> "For from within, out of the heart of man, come evil thoughts, sexual immorality, theft, murder, adultery, coveting, wickedness, deceit, sensuality, envy, slander, pride, foolishness. All these evil things come from within, and they defile a person." (Mark 7:21-23)

To be true to yourself is the very heart of sin. So don't be captured by false disqualifications.

False wisdom

Finally, don't be captured by false wisdom, or by the mere appearance of wisdom:

> If with Christ you died to the elemental spirits of the world, why, as if you were still alive in the world, do you submit to regulations—"Do not handle, Do not

taste, Do not touch" (referring to things that all perish as they are used)—according to human precepts and teachings? These have indeed an appearance of wisdom in promoting self-made religion and asceticism and severity to the body, but they are of no value in stopping the indulgence of the flesh. (2:20-23)

Here are the 'elements of this world' writ large—the lies and foundational principles of thinking that undergird this dark world. This often takes the form of self-made religion that forbids our senses from sensing—except, of course, for the sense of pain.

Heresies like this are often 'godly heresies'. That is, self-made religious rituals almost always start with a desire to obey God, to be pure, and to be like God in some way. These are good desires. After all, Jesus taught that to follow him is to *deny* yourself and take up your cross (Mark 8:34).

In the fourth century, an English monk called Pelagius denied the Bible's doctrines of original sin and total depravity. What drove Pelagius to these heretical views was his godly desire to see moral transformation in the people around him. He wanted people to do good and he took the view that the Augustinian (and biblical) idea of original sin removed any sense of human responsibility. He believed this kept people from making any effort towards doing good.

Original sin

Original sin is a term used to describe one aspect of the Bible's teaching about human sinfulness. As descendants of Adam, all human beings are born with a sinful nature. When Adam rebelled against God, he did so as our representative or 'head' in such a way that we share in his guilt and—apart from Christ—stand condemned before God. Another way to put it is that we are not born with a neutral nature (from which point we all just happen to choose sin), but rather we are born as sinners, already standing condemned as part of the human race that is descended from Adam and is therefore 'in Adam'. The only way to escape God's judgement is by turning to Jesus, which means we are now 'in Christ'. A key passage on 'original sin' is Romans 5:12-21.

In other words, he chose a form of self-made religion—a belief system that relied on human wisdom, rather than on the wisdom of God as revealed in the gospel of Jesus.

In our own day and age, the Roman Catholic approach to religion is what we might call 'Semi-Pelagian'. While Pelagianism teaches that we are saved *only* by what we do, Semi-Pelagianism teaches that we are saved *both* by what Jesus did for us *and* by what we do—as opposed to the Bible, which teaches that we are saved *only* by what Jesus did for us.

False teachers, as described in the Bible, don't tend to wake up in the morning thinking to themselves, "I'll destroy the church of God if it's the last thing I do!" They often set out with godly motives and good intentions—like Pelagius and like our Roman Catholic friends. But sadly, regardless of motives, false teaching is always wrong. Don't be captured by false teachers. It will often take great courage, resolve and clarity to avoid being captured by false ideas and false teaching.

Mahae was an Ethiopian evangelist who faithfully proclaimed Christ for many years. During his life, he was imprisoned at least 33 times and often beaten for preaching the gospel. On one occasion, Mahae and over 50 other Christians had been arrested for refusing to follow the unbiblical rituals that were imposed by local Orthodox priests. As they were led to the courthouse with chains around their wrists and shackles around their ankles, Mahae and his Christian brothers and sisters sang praises to Jesus:

> We follow Jesus Christ—we follow him!
> Creator of the world—we follow him!
> Jesus Christ the Lord—we follow him!
> He died and rose again—we follow him!
> All the way he leads us—we follow him!

When an Orthodox priest accused the Christians of not fasting, Mahae replied, "But we do fast. We fast from sin!"[30]

Knowing Jesus Christ and resolving to follow Jesus Christ allowed Mahae to reject false disqualifications and the mere appearance of human wisdom, to escape the shadows and to continue to walk in Christ—even when it cost him everything.

Remember, the best defence against being taken captive by hollow and deceptive philosophy or by empty deceit is to see Christ clearly, know him deeply and to remember your union with him. "Therefore, as you received Christ Jesus the

---

30 Richard McLellan, *Warriors of Ethiopia*, Lost Coin Books, UK, 2013, pp. 25-32.

Lord, so walk in him, rooted and built up in him and established in the faith, just as you were taught, abounding in thanksgiving."

Give thanks and pray

- Spend some time giving thanks to God for all his goodness to you—especially giving thanks that he has provided his Son, the Lord Jesus, as our Saviour.
- Pray that God would help you to know Jesus more and more deeply.
- Pray that God would help you to turn away from the elements of this world.
- Give thanks for the witness of other Christians who have held fast to Jesus, no matter what the cost.

Discussion questions

- How can you nurture your walk in Christ and be rooted and built up in him?
- What can help you to abound in thanksgiving?
- Are there any philosophies that threaten to take you away from Christ? If so, how can you guard against them?

5 | Raised with Christ

I f you were to walk onto the campus of Wollongong University, you would find yourself in the 'heavenly places' of the Illawarra region of New South Wales, Australia. This campus is so beautiful that some have thought it's an extension of the Botanical Gardens across the road. There are ponds where eels swim and ducks frolic. There are fields with deer roaming free. There are restaurants, cafes, a cinema, a hair salon and a pool in which both the Finnish and American swimming teams trained in preparation for the Olympic Games.

But perhaps most inspirationally of all, you will find this slogan written on banners sprawling all across the campus: "Find Your Why".

To the modern mind, here is the real reason that Wollongong University is so heavenly: it's a place to Find Your *Why*. It presents itself as a place to discover the very reason for your existence—a place to find your identity, a place where you may even find "all the treasures of wisdom and knowledge".

But as we have seen in Colossians, such wisdom is so 'elementary'. This kind of thinking is in accord with "the elemental spirits of the world, and not according to Christ".

Our real 'why' is that we exist in, through and for the one in whom "all the treasures of wisdom and know-ledge" are really found: Jesus Christ alone. "As you received Christ Jesus the Lord, so walk in him, rooted and built up in him and established in the faith, just as you were taught, abounding in thanksgiving." We have died with Jesus, been buried with Jesus and been *raised* with Jesus. This is your why.

So if the skies peeled open and we could gaze into heaven itself, what would we see? We would see the risen Jesus, the man in whom all the fullness of deity dwells bodily, seated next to his heavenly Father.

Do you believe this? As chapter 3 of Colossians begins, Paul argues that to believe that Christ has been raised will genuinely transform your life. For every Christian has been united to Jesus, the preeminent one, who sits at God's right hand in heaven. You cannot get any closer to Jesus. Physically, you may be lying in bed or seated on a lounge chair as you read this book. But spiritually, you are seated with Christ in heaven:

> If then you have been raised with Christ, seek the things that are above, where Christ is, seated at the right hand of God. Set your minds on things that are above, not on things that are on earth. For you have died, and your life is hidden with Christ in God. When Christ who is your life appears, then you also will appear with him in glory. (3:1-4)

Christians are dual citizens of heaven and earth. We are united to Jesus, and yet we are to seek Jesus. We don't have to seek Jesus in the sense that he's hiding from us—playing a cosmic game of hide 'n' seek. Rather, we are to seek him in the sense of setting our minds and hearts on where we truly are, the place where he is seated: heaven. We are to seek to live a heavenly life now, even as we remain on earth.

Imagine you're getting ready to migrate to Japan. You'll naturally set your mind on the things of Japan. You might do this by *seeking* to eat sushi, watch sumo wrestling and learn Japanese. You'd think about life in Japan and set your heart on Japanese things.

In the same way, we are to set our heart on heavenly things and on the things of Christ. We are to think about where we really are: with Christ, in the heavenly realms. Your life is hidden with Christ, so much so that Paul can even say Christ *is* your life. And if your life is hidden with Christ who is in heaven, then that's where your mind should also be—longing for his return and pursuing the things of heaven, even as you continue to live on earth.

You don't have to "find your why". God has given us our 'why'. It revolves entirely around Christ. He is the centre of our solar system and the orienting centre of everything we do. Our priorities, our family life, our church life, our leisure life, our sex life, our speech life—everything in life revolves around the resurrected Christ, who is in heaven.

Murdering sin with pleasure

So as those raised with Christ, we must be committed to murdering everything that is not heavenly in our lives: sin.

> When Christ who is your life appears, then you also will appear with him in glory.
>
> Put to death therefore what is earthly in you: sexual immorality, impurity, passion, evil desire, and covetousness, which is idolatry. On account of these the wrath of God is coming. (3:4-6)

Jesus' death and resurrection have power to transform our sex lives. In his excellent commentary on Colossians, John Woodhouse argues persuasively that the terms "impurity, passion, evil desire and covetousness" are, in this context, all used to describe perversions of godly sexuality.[31] These are all different types or different aspects of sexual immorality, with "evil desire" referring to wrong sexual desire and "covetousness" referring to an uncontrolled desire for more and more sexual immorality.

Overcoming such powerful sin will require great power. But this power cannot come from my own innate moral fibre. The power to murder sin can only come from a resolve that is fueled by the pleasure of being "raised with Christ".

Rosaria Butterfield is a former English professor who lived in a lesbian relationship for many years, championing the ideals of the LGBTQ movement and being at the forefront of the movement through her teaching position on a major US college campus. But she came to know Jesus through the faithful ministry of an 'Epaphras' in her local church. Since then, she has clearly and courageously proclaimed the gospel and has spoken about biblical sexuality

31   Woodhouse, *Colossians and Philemon*, pp. 189-91.

in articles, churches, books and universities.[32]

Since her conversion, Butterfield says she has met countless people for whom every relationship has been marred by sexual sin. This includes wives whose husbands are addicted to pornography, husbands whose wives have left them for lesbian lovers, teenagers sending and receiving explicit text messages, best friends who frequent cyber-sex sites together, cousins in sexual relationships, homeschooled children who found violent pornography on their mothers' mobile phones, and much more besides.

Clearly, sexual sin is rampant. And in a culture that values individual freedom, pleasure, self-expression and 'being true to yourself' as much as ours does, it's hard to see any way to turn back the tide.

Does any of this sexual sin come close to your world? Any of it at all?

If so, where do we go with problems of this magnitude? How do we begin to handle such deadly sin? As Rosaria Butterfield writes:

> I find the words of the Puritan Elias Pledger to be a great comfort: "I will lay the weight of my sinking spirit on the free grace of Christ." They tell me that, even as I wrestle with my sin, I need to cling more to Christ than to my feelings... Every time I embrace the means of grace, every time I read the Word of God and it convicts me of sin, and every time I respond with God's wisdom in repentance and confession of

32 See especially Rosaria Butterfield, *The Secret Thoughts of an Unlikely Convert: An English Professor's Journey into Christian Faith*, Crown & Covenant, Pittsburgh, PA, 2012.

sin... I am risen from the tomb and resurrected into the light by the power of Jesus Christ himself, who declares to me that there is no condemnation for me any longer, because I am clothed in his righteousness by the power of his resurrection.[33]

To put it another way, the power to kill sexual immorality is fueled by the understanding that I am raised with Christ. So now, I am to be a murderer. I am to put such things to death.

But I find this hard.

We so often drift into the things of this world rather than plunging into them. The sexual offender usually doesn't become a sexual offender overnight. It invariably begins with a thousand small, bad decisions: a little late-night TV, then a few graphic movies, then internet pornography, then violent internet pornography...

Put sin to death *early*. Kill it! Have zero tolerance for sexual sin of any kind. If you're a Christian living for heaven and seeking the things of Christ, sexual sin makes no sense. Deal with it now. As John Owen famously said, "Be killing sin or it will be killing you".[34]

The very best way to kill transient, worldly, ungodly, damaging pleasure is with eternal pleasure. As John Piper has rightly pointed out, "No-one sins out of duty. We sin

---

33 Rosaria Butterfield, *Openness Unhindered: Further Thoughts of an Unlikely Convert on Sexual Identity and Union with Christ*, Kindle edn, Crown & Covenant, Pittsburgh, PA, 2015, chapter 2.

34 John Owen, *Of the Mortification of Sin in Believers*, Christian Classics Ethereal Library, Grand Rapids, MI, p. 10. Available online (viewed 19 December 2018): www.ccel.org/ccel/owen/mort.pdf.

because it holds out some promise of happiness."[35] But the more we focus on heaven, the more we consider Christ and set our minds on the beautiful, holy things that are above, the more we will see the ugliness of our sin, and the more we will be motivated to kill it. For the pleasure of being raised with Christ truly outweighs any pleasure on earth.

So the solution to sin, sexual or otherwise, is not to remove our desire for pleasure, but to renew our pleasures.

Consider the example of a student I know—a young man who formerly enjoyed the pleasure of sleeping in. But suddenly, he was awake and jogging every morning at 6am. Why? He met a girl, and she also jogged every morning at 6am. My friend had found a new pleasure.

Seeking Christ in heaven means we have found a new pleasure. We can kill sexually immoral pleasure with resurrection pleasure.

Killing ungodly speech

Furthermore, living for heaven will involve putting away not just ungodly sexual activity, but also ungodly speech:

> But now you must put them all away: anger, wrath, malice, slander, and obscene talk from your mouth. Do not lie to one another... (3:8-9a)

Perhaps the phrase that best captures all these behaviours is found in verse 8: "from your mouth".[36] Just as the idea of

---

35 John Piper, *Future Grace: The Purifying Power of the Promises of God*, Multnomah, Colorado Springs, CO, 2012, p. 1.

36 cf. John Woodhouse, *Colossians & Philemon*, p. 192.

sexual immorality tinges all that has come before, so now the idea of ungodly speaking tinges everything in these verses. For is that not how your anger and malice is almost always expressed—through ungodly speech?

If you have a problem with your temper, put it away. There is, of course, a right kind of anger. Jesus, for example, became angry in Mark 3:5, and Paul says, "Be angry and do not sin" (Eph 4:26), *not* "never be angry". It's possible to possess and express anger rightly. But it's rare. And sinning in anger is almost always expressed in our speech.

The way that we speak to one another is so important. Sharp words, sarcasm, slander or even humour used to subtly put down someone else can all be devastating—whether it's face to face, behind someone's back or online via social media.

After moving from Malaysia to Australia as a boy, it took me a while to learn that, in Australian culture, putting someone down can be a sign of affection. The longer I lived in Australia, the more I started speaking this way in order to fit in. But I started to go too far. And one day I knew I had gone way too far as a teenager when, because of my sharp words, someone came up and hit me in the face. That's how much our words can hurt one another.

As well as putting away

Five rules for social media: THINK

Given the danger of misusing our words, can I suggest that you stop and THINK before you write anything on any social media platform? Ask yourself these five questions:

Is it **T**ruthful?
Is it **H**elpful?
Is it **I**nformative?
Is it **N**ecessary?
Is it **K**ind?

How many dispiriting arguments could be avoided—and how many posts would never need to be written at all—if we applied these rules?

malicious words, we're also to put away obscene language, which is inconsistent with living for heaven.

In 1904 and 1905, God saved around 150,000 people in what came to be known as the Welsh Revival. Among them were many coal miners, who were said to be among the most foul-mouthed people on earth. But after Christ and his salvation spread through these communities, one biography described the change this way:

> Soul winning spread through the coalmines. Profane swearing stopped. Productivity in the mines increased. Even the pit ponies were confused by the change in their masters' behaviour, as coaxing replaced kicking and cursing.[37]

Putting on the new self

All these transformations—including our sex lives and our speech lives—flow from having put on the heavenly clothing of Christ:

> Do not lie to one another, seeing that you have put off the old self with its practices and have put on the new self, which is being renewed in knowledge after the image of its creator. (3:9-10)

Note where this renewal starts: with *knowledge*. God renews us with knowledge, through the Scriptures, which reveal his will to us. He renews our minds and refocuses them on

37 R Cargill, '"A Godly Heritage" (45): The Welsh Revival of 1904-05', *Believer's Magazine*, October 2016 (viewed 19 December 2018): www.believersmagazine.com/bm.php?i=20161003.

whatever is true, and honourable, and just, and pure, and lovely, and commendable, and excellent, and worthy of praise (cf. Phil 4:8).

Also, note the tense used here: we *are being renewed*. Even though we are already a new creation, and even though we have already put off the old self and put on the new self, we are not instantly renewed—at least not in an absolute sense. It will take a lifetime of renewal in the knowledge of Christ and his place in the universe, so that he becomes the pulsating centre of our lives. Remember Paul's prayer back in chapter 1: "we have not ceased to pray for you, asking that you may be filled with the knowledge of his will in all spiritual wisdom and understanding..." (1:9). This renewal involves being recreated as the humanity we were meant to be—like Jesus.

But what is verse 11 doing here? "Here there is not Greek and Jew, circumcised and uncircumcised, barbarian, Scythian, slave, free; but Christ is all, and in all." It seems an awkward transition from verse 10, almost as though it could be left out entirely. But this verse is crucial, because it forms part of the subterranean reservoir that keeps feeding this entire text: namely, the crucial doctrine of our union with Christ.

In context, "Christ is all" means that Christ is all that matters. He is the beloved Son in, through and for whom all things were made. He is the head of the church and the one who reconciles all things to himself. He is Lord. He is all that matters.

And he is not only all, but he is also *in* all. He is *in* all Christians because of our union with him. And this is wonderfully inclusive and comprehensive. Christ is in all Christians—whether they are Jewish or Gentile, Australian or American, single or married, student or worker, doctor or doorman, young or old. He is in all Christians whether they are same-sex attracted, gender-confused, have had an abortion or struggle with pornography.

No matter who you are, if you have received Christ Jesus as Lord, then you have been filled in him, you have died and been buried with him, you have been raised with him, and you will appear with him when he comes in glory. This, and nothing else, is the most important thing about you. Your identity is found in him.

Think of the power of the idea that Christ is *in you*. Think, for example, about who is present when you are alone and tempted to watch pornography or to stay up too late with someone who is not your spouse. Christ is in that bedroom. Christ is in that car.

Think about who is present when you're tempted to drink that extra beer or that extra glass of wine. Think about who is present when you're tempted to slander someone—especially on social media.

This can all seem too hard. Overcoming our sin can seem so overwhelming. But as John Owen wrote, "Our greatest hindrance in the Christian life is not our lack of effort, but our lack of acquaintedness with our privileges".[38] As we become more acquainted with the privilege of being in Christ, this will enable us not only to turn away from the ungodly behaviours of our past, but also to start clothing ourselves in the good works that are fitting for citizens of heaven.

---

38 Quoted by Ian Hamilton, 'God is Trinity', *Cambridge Presbyterian Church*, July 2015 (viewed 10 December 2018): www.cambridgepres.org. uk/resources/app/type/pastors-blog/resource/2140/title/god-is-trinity.

"Put on then, as God's chosen ones, holy and beloved…" (3:12a). What incredible privileges! Just like the Colossians, we are "chosen ones". Among all the people in the world, God chose you and me to be among his people. We are 'holy'. We are 'saints', set apart from sin and set apart for God, because we are in Christ. And we are 'beloved'. Just as Jesus is beloved, so are we, because we are in Christ. God could not love us any more than he does.

How well are you acquainted with these privileges? For example, has it occurred to you that, if you have received Christ Jesus as Lord, then you are among the most privileged people on the face of the whole earth? You know God as your Father, Jesus as your Saviour and friend, every Christian as your brother or sister, and heaven as your home. Bathe in the heavenly privileges that are yours in Christ.

And if all these things are true, then who should we be?

> Put on then, as God's chosen ones, holy and beloved, compassionate hearts, kindness, humility, meekness, and patience, bearing with one another and, if one has a complaint against another, forgiving each other; as the Lord has forgiven you, so you also must forgive. (3:12-13)

The virtues listed in these verses are all virtues of the Lord Jesus Christ himself. It's another way of saying "put on the Lord Jesus Christ" (Rom 13:14; cf. Gal 3:27). Jesus showed compassion when he cried over Jerusalem (Luke 19:41). He showed kindness to the sinful woman who anointed his feet with ointment (and with her tears, Luke 7:37-38). He displayed perfect humility when he emptied himself and took on the form of a servant (Phil 2:5-8). He is patient with us in desiring our repentance. And he forgives us—not just seven times, but "seventy-seven times" (Matt 18:22), meaning he forgives us incalculably and without limit through his blood shed on the cross. To put on all these virtues is to put on Christ himself.

But supremely, to put on Christ is to live a life of love: "And above all these put on love, which binds everything together in perfect harmony" (3:14). Love is the supreme virtue that will live on into the new creation, because God himself is love.

Graham Staines was an Australian missionary who spent 35 years helping the poor and illiterate in India. He served as Director of the Leprosy Mission in Orissa and helped translate the New Testament into the language of the Ho tribe. In 1999, while attending an annual camp, Graham slept in a jeep with his two sons—Philip, aged ten, and Timothy, aged six. Just after midnight on 23rd January, Hindu extremists smashed the windows of the jeep, filled the car with gasoline and set it alight. Later that morning, the charred bodies of Graham and his sons were found embracing one another.

Graham was survived by his wife, Gladys, and his then-13-year-old daughter, Esther. In 2006, Esther was studying medicine at an Australian university and I had the enormous privilege of meeting her at a student conference. When she was interviewed in front of the entire conference, she spoke of how she had forgiven her family's murderers, and indeed prayed for them. She added, "I don't know how, or where, or when, but it is my desire to return to India to speak of the forgiveness that is offered in Jesus". Esther is now married with children, but her desire to forgive has not changed.

Love like that is supernatural. It only comes from

someone who has put on Christ, is clothed in his compassion, and is transformed by his love.

If ever there are virtues to put on, they are the virtues of Christ himself. But how can we work on clothing ourselves in these virtues? Perhaps it all just seems too hard. You might be exhausted from parenting young children. Maybe you've taken too many body blows as you've tried to serve in your local church. Maybe family and friends are slow to change and hard to love. Maybe you've been offended in a way that is so damaging that it just feels impossible to forgive.

With all that and more going on, how can 'becoming like Jesus' be more than a pious platitude? How can it become the reality of our lives?

First, begin by focusing again on the Lord Jesus Christ. Who is he? How did he live? Remember, this is the man who, in the midst of being crucified, prayed, "Father, forgive them, for they know not what they do" (Luke 23:34).

Second, remember that Christ is *in you*. Meditate on your union with him. Acquaint yourself more and more deeply with the privileges that are yours *in him*.

Thirdly, practice these virtues. Simply get into the habit of living and acting this way. Dare I say, 'Just Do It'.

That may sound overly simplistic, so let me give an example. How will you practice patience? Start by working out what causes you stress, then work out a strategy to deal with it. Make sure your strategy begins with prayer, but work out what other steps you can take. For example, I know that I am always extra tired when I arrive home from a conference. Tiredness breeds impatience. So, in the first few hours after I arrive back home, I need to work extra hard to care for my wife and children. As I stand at the front door, I pray for patience.

Apply the same kind of thinking to other virtues: compassion, humility, meekness and forbearance. Work through the list, considering what causes you to fall into sin and how you can develop a plan to walk in holiness. As you do this, dwell on who God is and on the privileges that are yours in Christ—and know that, in Christ, we *can* change. It may take some time. No-one said that changing to become like Jesus would be easy. But it is possible, and it will be worth it.

The peace of Christ

Paul then finishes this section of the letter with three wonderful commands:

> And let the peace of Christ rule in your hearts, to which indeed you were called in one body. And be thankful. Let the word of Christ dwell in you richly, teaching and admonishing one another in all wisdom, singing psalms and hymns and spiritual songs, with thankfulness in your hearts to God. And whatever you do, in word or deed, do everything in the name of the Lord Jesus, giving thanks to God the Father through him. (3:15-17)

The "peace of Christ" that Paul has in mind must allude back to 1:20. This is the peace of 'true order' that only comes through the cross, a peace that shapes how we relate to one another.

The next command, in verse 16, provides the means of letting this peace rule in our hearts. We are to bathe ourselves in the gospel as we read, speak and sing the Scriptures to one another. The Bible is the means by which we "let the peace of Christ rule in [our] hearts".

Rosaria Butterfield straddled two lives for two years: one as a lesbian lover and the other as someone who read her Bible regularly. Here's how she describes the transformation she experienced:

> After years and years of this something happened. The Bible got to be bigger inside me than I. It overflowed into my world. And then one Sunday morning, two years after I first met Ken [her pastor] and Floy [Ken's wife] and two years after I started reading the Bible for my research, I left the bed I shared with my lesbian partner and an hour later I showed up in a pew at the Syracuse Reformed Presbyterian Church... I kept going back to church to hear more sermons. I had made friendships with people in the church by this time and I had really appreciated the way that they talked about the sermons throughout the week, how the Word of God dwelt in them, and how they referenced it in the details of their days.[39]

Isn't this a beautiful picture of letting the word of Christ "dwell in us richly"? Isn't this a glorious picture of how the Bible transforms lives, and of how one transformed life can impact another? Isn't it a joy to hear of God's people "teaching one another"? As a preacher, let me assure you that there is no greater joy than to realize God's people aren't relying on me—but to know that they are "teaching and admonishing one another in all wisdom". Isn't this the picture we

---

39 Rosaria Butterfield, 'After Darkness, Light', *Ligonier Ministries*, 2015 (viewed 19 December 2018): www.ligonier.org/learn/conferences/after-darkness-light-2015-national-conference/repentance-renewal/.

long to see played out in all our churches and all our gospel ministries?

Granted, this is easier said than done. As the saying goes: "To live above with those you love: Undiluted Glory. To live below with those you know: that's another story." One day, we will love one another perfectly. Until then, expect this to be hard work.

But the situation is not hopeless; there is something we can do. Did you notice the big idea behind Paul's final command in this section? Look again: "Whatever you do, in word or deed, do everything in the name of the Lord Jesus, giving thanks to God the Father through him" (3:17).

All that we do—our thoughts, our words and our deeds—should be done to promote the reputation of Jesus. And this only makes sense if Christ is in us. But here is the big idea behind the command: although there is a lifetime of renewal lying ahead of us all, and although we strive for perfection while knowing that we'll never achieve it in this life, we can always *be thankful*. No matter what we are going through, we can always find reason to give thanks to God—whether it's simply for another breath or another heartbeat, or for deeper realities such as knowing that our Creator loves us dearly even as we endure pain and agony.

The renewal we long for may be slow, but it will be real. And it all arises from being raised with Christ. This is not just 'pie in the sky when you die'; it's more like 'meat as a treat when you eat' (unless you're a vegetarian). Jesus' resurrection transforms our eternity, but it also transforms our lives now as we live out our union with him and remember the privileges that are ours in him. This is where you "find your why".

CS Lewis wrote:

> If you read history you will find that the Christians who did most for the present world were just those who thought most of the next... It is since Christians have largely ceased to think of the other world that they have become so ineffective in this.[40]

Do you want to make a difference to the world? Do you want to make an impact for God? Do you want to "find your why"? Then set your mind on things above.

Give thanks and pray

- Give thanks that we can live this life knowing that we are 'in Christ'.
- Pray that God would help you to navigate all the experiences of life with thankfulness.
- Pray that God would help you to kill any remaining sin with the heavenly pleasure of being 'in Christ'.

Discussion questions

- What prevents you from setting your mind on heavenly things?
- What besetting sins do you need to put to death?
- How can you nurture a heavenly mindset to do so?

40 CS Lewis, *Mere Christianity*, Harper Collins, New York, 2001, p. 134.

6 | Order in Christ

We live in difficult and confusing times. Voluntary euthanasia, abortion, no-fault divorce and the redefinition of marriage are now woven into the social fabric of most Western nations. Our children and our grandchildren will have to navigate a climate where the 'elements of the world' dictate the social and political agendas.

But, of course, this is not unique to the 21st century Western world. Between the death and resurrection of Jesus and his return in glory, we live in what the Bible calls the 'last days'. And the New Testament couldn't be clearer about the challenges of the Christian life in these 'last days': "But understand this, that in the last days there will come times of difficulty" (2 Tim 3:1). That's how Paul put it near the end of his life, in a letter to his friend and protégé, Timothy. He went on to say that many people will be "lovers of self" and "lovers of pleasure rather than lovers of God" (2 Tim 3:2, 4).

As such, the domain of darkness in which we live is no darker than the days of the first century, when Paul wrote to the Colossians. We live in the *same* last days.

That's why the gospel is so breathtaking. In his death and resurrection, Jesus brings about true order by reconciling all things to himself. The gospel unites us to Jesus, the beloved Son. And the gospel reorders our love lives (as we saw in the previous chapter) by transforming our sex lives, our speech lives, our character and our relationships.

This is all part and parcel of what Paul had in mind back in 2:5: "For though I am absent in body, yet I am with you in spirit, rejoicing to see your *good order* and the firmness of your faith in Christ". The "good order" in which Paul rejoices is that which Christ brings as he reconciles all things to himself and as he enables us to live transformed lives as we set our minds on things above. And faith in Christ brings about good order in two specific areas: within family life and even within the institution of slavery.

But if we're honest, many of us feel a sense of awkwardness as we read some of these words:

> Wives, submit to your husbands, as is fitting in the Lord. Husbands, love your wives, and do not be harsh with them. Children, obey your parents in everything, for this pleases the Lord. Fathers, do not provoke your children, lest they become discouraged. Bondservants, obey in everything those who are your earthly masters… (3:18-22a)

This is part of the timeless "word of Christ" which is supposed to "dwell in [us] richly" (3:16). But I wonder whether this part of the word of Christ dwells in us *reluctantly*. As you prepare to work through this chapter, why not stop at this point and pray that God would move your heart from reluctant acceptance to rich reception? For these verses spell out

God's ideal for some of our most important relationships.

If there is to be good order, God commands us to submit to others in various relationships. The word 'submit' simply means to place yourself under the authority of another or to order yourself under someone else. But I am acutely aware that for many 21st century people the call to submit sounds bizarre or even wrong. There are some who would like to eradicate the word 'submission' from the English language altogether, believing that it conveys injustice, inequality or the removal of human rights. The idea of 'headship' attracts the very same objections for the very same reasons.

For some, submission has even become part of what philosophers call a 'defeater belief'. A defeater belief is the idea that if 'Belief A' is true, then 'Belief B' cannot be true. In our culture, which values individual freedom above almost anything else, 'Belief A' is: "Submitting yourself to someone else would be foolish and wrong". Therefore, 'Belief B' (i.e. the Bible) must be wrong when it calls on one person to submit to another. The very notion of submission makes Christianity seem implausible and unbelievable.

Before going any further and attempting to defend the notion of submission, let me say very clearly: If you are the victim of any kind of abuse that has taken place

Confronting defeater beliefs

What are some common defeater beliefs that might prevent a person today from considering the gospel (for example, around submission, sexuality, the nature of truth, relationships, science or freedom)? Spend some time pondering how you could address some of these defeater beliefs when you encounter them among friends, family or colleagues. Pray that God would give you boldness and opportunities to speak.

in the name of 'submission' or 'headship', I am very, very sorry. There is absolutely no place for a sinful distortion of headship or submission that results in abuse of any kind, whether it's in marriage, in the wider family, in the church or anywhere in society—no place!

However, the ultimate solution is not to erase any notion of order, headship or submission. Rather, it is to erase all *sinful* notions of order, headship and submission, and instead to embrace a *Christ-saturated* notion of order—one that revolves around him, his Lordship, his kindness, his compassion, his humility and his love. The virtues of Christ himself must transform how we see all expressions of order in our relationships.

A Christ-saturated family life

Let me make four preliminary comments.

First, if you are single, separated or divorced—or if you are a victim of abuse (as a sister *or* as a brother)—I want to acknowledge the pain you may feel as I write for wives and husbands directly. Please know that you are not forgotten. My earnest prayer is that God would comfort and encourage you as you consider this part of his word, and that you will find it a balm for your soul despite your difficult circumstances.

Second, a word on forgiveness. I touched briefly on forgiveness in the previous chapter, but the whole topic is worth a chapter (or an entire book!) on its own. My own view is that to forgive (as the Lord forgave you) should involve repentance on the part of anyone who has wronged you, for the Lord forgives those who repent. However, as those in Christ, we (like our Lord) must always have a forgiving *stance*, not nurturing resentment or anger—even if there is no repentance in the one who has aggrieved you. Even if we are innocent victims, we should long to forgive like Jesus, who prayed, "Father, forgive them, for they know not what they do" (Luke 23:34). That way, even if there is no repentance from the guilty party, we will not be overcome by the poison of bitterness.

Third, it goes without saying that our relationships are complex and even the best marriage is between two sinful people. So we all need to hear what God says when he speaks of his ideal for marriage and family.

Fourth, given our current climate, and given the particular areas in

What is forgiveness?

I am acutely aware that there are differences in opinion regarding the word 'forgiveness' in the Scriptures (given the semantic range of the word). What I define as 'a forgiving *stance*' is what others define as 'forgiveness'. It is to erase someone's sins against us by assuming the burden of debt, and to seek *not* to harbour bitterness or resentment, whether the wrongdoer has repented or not. Such a stance comes at great cost to the person wronged, although that cost is only a microscopic measure of what our Lord Jesus experienced on the cross.[41]

which I see many Christians struggle to obey these verses, I would prefer to address husbands first. But because the *text* begins by addressing wives, I'll begin by addressing wives too.

41 For differing views on this, see Chris Brauns' *Unpacking Forgiveness* (Crossway, Wheaton, 2008), and Mark Baddeley's series of 8 articles starting with 'Forgiveness and repentance (part 1): A survey of the landscape' (*The Briefing*, 6 July 2010: www.matthiasmedia.com/briefing/2010/07/forgiveness-and-repentance-part-1-a-survey-of-the-landscape/).

So, with those four preliminary comments in mind, let's start by looking at God's good word to wives (or would-be wives).

"Wives, submit to your husbands"

"Wives, submit to your husbands, as is fitting in the Lord." (3:18)

To be "fitting" is to be Jesus-like, to be in 'good order'. As such, the kind of submission Paul describes is *voluntary*. After all, Jesus voluntarily submitted to his Father's will.

Moreover, submitting to his Father's will did not make Jesus unequal to his Father, since he is fully God—just as submitting to a police officer doesn't make you unequal to him or her, since you are both fully human. But it is 'fitting' to submit to the authority of the police, and it is 'fitting' for Jesus to submit to his Father. And so, as a wife, if you choose to submit to your husband, it does not mean you are unequal to him.

Submission does not mean that you become a doormat. It does not mean you now have no opinions of your own. It does not mean you can't differ from your husband or even be critical in your thinking. It does not mean you're bound to the kitchen or that you are at his beck and call or that you are owned by him as a piece of his property.

Furthermore, it would be 'unfitting in the Lord' to submit to your husband if he wanted you to do anything that is clearly not pleasing to God, as revealed in his word. In fact, if you feel this is your situation, please seek help.

So what *does* fitting submission involve? It means

willingly honouring your husband as God's appointed head over you and rejoicing in your husband's initiative to serve you—just as Jesus did with his Father.

For Paul, fitting submission involves 'respect', for it is very difficult to submit to your husband if you don't respect him. This is certainly clear from what Paul says as part of a longer description of submission within marriage in Ephesians 5: "Let each one of you love his wife as himself, and let the wife see that she respects her husband" (Eph 5:33).

It's good for a bride's marriage vows to include the promise to respect her husband. And don't worry—I'm about to address husbands *very clearly* on how they must love their wives. But may I first ask those of you who are wives: Do you respect your husband as is fitting in the Lord?

I asked my wife, Jeanette, to consider what she would like to say to wives (or would-be wives) on this topic and she had much wonderful wisdom to share. You can read her insights at the end of the chapter.

"Husbands, love your wives"

What about God's good word to husbands?

> "Husbands, love your wives, and do not be harsh with them." (3:19)

What does it mean to love your wife? Paul doesn't explain it in any detail here, but he explains a husband's love for his wife more extensively in Ephesians 5:

> Husbands, love your wives, as Christ loved the church and gave himself up for her, that he might sanctify

her, having cleansed her by the washing of water with the word, so that he might present the church to himself in splendour, without spot or wrinkle or any such thing, that she might be holy and without blemish. In the same way husbands should love their wives as their own bodies. He who loves his wife loves himself. (Eph 5:25-28)

If you are a husband, you are to love your wife *in the same way* that Christ loved the church. This means that, like Jesus, you are to move heaven and earth—and hell—and sacrifice everything for her good. If that means literally dying for her, so be it. If you need to sacrifice your life for her good, do it. That doesn't make you Superman; you're just doing your job. Death is what it's all about. Don't get married if you're not ready to lay down your life for your bride. The shape of marriage for husbands is the shape of the cross.

Your responsibility is to care for her, nurture her and protect her as if she were your own body. That will mean, at the very least, sacrificing your own interests and desires for her sake. And if you physically harm your wife in any way whatsoever, it means (among other things) that you are mentally unwell. For as far as Paul is concerned, hurting your wife is akin to committing an act of self-harm.

So what will it look like to love your wife as Christ loved the church in practice? Let me share four points.

First, *value her as your equal*. First Peter 3:7 says that your wife is an "heir with you of the grace of life". You may be God's appointed head within the marriage, but—much more importantly—she is your co-heir in Christ. It is vital that your wife feels properly valued.

Second, *cherish* your wife. Cherish your wife by helping her to *feel* loved. It's one thing to love your wife. It's quite another thing to help her *feel* loved. Ask her: what makes her feel loved? Do your homework; the answers might surprise you. Once you find out the answers, make some plans. Roll up your sleeves and make an effort. Actively look for ways to cherish your wife.

Third, try to *make submission a joy* for your wife. Some of these kinds of statements might help:

"Darling, please let me take the garbage out."
"Please let me change our baby's nappy."
"How about I cook dinner tonight?"
"Let me take you shopping."
"Let me turn off the game and watch your favourite show with you instead."

We may smile or laugh as we read some of those comments, but over a long period of time these kinds of simple, heartfelt gestures can make a big difference and can help to create an environment where submission is a joy.

Fourth, take the initiative to plan how you can nourish your wife spiritually, emotionally and physically. For example, how can you read the Bible with her? If it's difficult to read the Bible together, work out how you can help your wife to read the Bible on her own or how you can help her to sit under great Bible teaching. For example, do you expect her to take the little ones out to creche at church each week or are you willing to take just as many turns on the roster? Whatever the case, nourish and cherish your wife spiritually. Nourish her physically, and nourish her emotionally. This will require sacrifice on your part. It takes planning, time and thought. But just as Christ sacrificed for his bride, so you must sacrifice for yours.

Husbands, love your wives—"and do not be harsh with them". Back in Colossians 3, Paul describes the opposite of loving your wife. To be harsh with your wife is to fail to love her as Jesus loved the church. It's to abuse your God-given headship. So let me make four pleas that will help ensure you are not harsh with your wife:

One: never leave the responsibility of raising the children to her alone. Raise your children together.

Two: never, ever demand that your wife submit to you, especially in the area of sex. Submission is voluntary and it is not for you to command.

Three: never think in terms of disciplining your wife. You should never discipline your wife. You discipline a child, but not your wife. She is your equal.

Four: **never** abuse your wife emotionally, physically or spiritually. At this point, we may be tempted to ask something like this: "What counts as abuse?" But can I suggest to you that even asking this question could imply that we have already sinned against our wives. Your every impulse should be to love, protect and cherish your bride. So instead, let me ask you this question: Is your wife afraid of you when you are angry? That should **never** be the case.

Husbands, love your wives, and do not be harsh with them. I beg you.

A word to children and fathers

Paul now turns from husbands and wives and delivers a command to children:

"Children, obey your parents in everything, for this pleases the Lord." (3:20)

Presumably, this command is for children who are old enough to understand what obedience means, since it is addressed to them. And yet, the implication of this command is that Paul is primarily addressing younger children, because they are to obey their parents "in everything". Parents have responsibility for the welfare of their children and this responsibility will be more comprehensive when the children are younger.

Again, no inequality is on view—children are just as human as their parents, bearing the image of God just as much as their parents. Their obedience simply reflects the God-given order that is best for the individuals, for the family, for the church and for society. Indeed, in 2 Timothy, Paul says that one of the signs of disordered lives and disordered relationships that characterize "the last days" will be children who are "disobedient to their parents" (2 Tim 3:2). That's why it pleases the Lord when children do obey their parents.

Parents, let me encourage you: make obedience understandable to your children. Make it a joy for them.

I asked my children for their advice at this point and here is what they shared:

Explain why you have certain rules. Why is a particular rule for your child's good? Why is the rule in place? Explain those things from the very beginning.

Help us to feel trusted. Help us to feel like you're on our side. There's a difference between saying, "You're not allowed to do that—and don't ask why" and saying, "I'm actually going to trust you with certain responsibilities". Extend some freedoms to your children in appropriate ways. For example, let them use that device or stay up a little late on the odd occasion, because you trust them and because you really are on their side. It will make their obedience more joyful.

Be honest with us. The example they gave me was based around the time my first wife, Bronwyn, was diagnosed with pancreatic cancer. Bronwyn and I were originally told that she had six months to live. We found this out at 1 o'clock in the morning and we told our children at breakfast the next day—through tears, and with much grief. But they are all so grateful that they knew from the very beginning, that nothing was hidden from them, and that we never thought, "We can't trust you with this information". They wanted (and needed) to hear the truth from us, despite the fact that it was devastatingly hard to have those conversations.

Children, obey your parents. But parents, make it as easy as possible for your children to obey.

And note the word that Paul now offers directly to fathers:

> "Do not provoke your children, lest they become discouraged." (3:21)

We who are fathers are not to discourage our children or to crush their spirits by saying harsh things. Words can scar for life.

When one of my daughters was much younger, we were riding our bicycles together. She was having fun and swerving her bike around, as children tend to do, and I was warning her to be careful so she didn't fall off. Predictably, she fell off. But rather than showing compassion and care, all I could manage was to get angry and say, "I told you so".

Just recently, we passed through the spot where this happened, so I asked her if she remembered. Straight away, she said yes—she remembered exactly what had happened. She was gracious about it and forgave me when I apologized, but harsh words are not easily forgotten.

In the more exasperating moments of parenthood, we who are fathers might wonder why the command isn't reversed: "children, do not provoke your fathers". But whatever frustrations our children might provoke in us pale in comparison to the lasting damage that our sharp words or our harsh treatment can do to them. Fathers, use your authority tenderly, lovingly and carefully. Do not provoke your children.

Slaves and masters

Having reflected on the family, Paul now turns to reflect on the institution of slavery. When we hear the word 'slavery', we usually think of the horrific slave trading ships that brought Africans to the Americas. But in the first century, slaves held all kinds of positions. In Rome alone, up to 80 or 90 per cent of the population were slaves or former slaves. No doubt many were abused, but there were also slaves who cared for the house or were even put in charge of running whole businesses—not unlike Joseph in Egypt (Gen 39:1-6).

Looking over the entire history of the human race, what's extraordinary is not so much that there has been slavery. What's extraordinary is that, in so many places, it has stopped. Almost every culture has included some form of slavery—sometimes as an economic reality and sometimes because of mere brutality. But slavery is an international phenomenon, not a white phenomenon.

The nation that played the biggest part in eradicating slavery was Great Britain—under the influence of the gospel. John Wesley wrote endless letters to Parliament in order to petition the government to abolish slavery. William Wilberforce, an evangelical Christian who helped found the Church Mission Society, used his position as the MP for Yorkshire to fight for an end to the slave trade. Almost without exception, the leaders of the abolitionist movement in the United States had become Christians during the second 'Great Awakening'.[42] And although it brought them no economic advantage to do so, Britain persuaded nation after nation to abolish slavery, even sending its warships to stop the trade.

The Bible doesn't condemn the institution of slavery as a whole, but neither does it endorse it. In fact, Paul encourages slaves to gain their freedom if they can (1 Cor 7:21). What the Bible very clearly condemns is the *abuse* of slavery and the *abuse* of slaves. Paul condemns 'enslavers', those who take others captive in order to sell them into slavery (1 Tim 1:10). And in our passage from Colossians, he addresses slaves at even greater length:

> Bondservants, obey in everything those who are your earthly masters, not by way of eye-service, as people-pleasers, but with sincerity of heart, fearing the Lord. Whatever you do, work heartily, as for the Lord and not for men, knowing that from the Lord you will

42 The second Great Awakening was a time of Christian revival from the late 18th century to the early or mid 19th century, leading to many new Christian converts having a positive influence on American society in numerous ways.

receive the inheritance as your reward. You are serving the Lord Christ. (3:22-24)

The Colossian church contained both slaves and masters. Given that Paul addresses slaves (or "bondservants") directly, it appears that they at least had freedom to attend church gatherings, possibly alongside their masters. Indeed, Onesimus (who we'll meet properly in 4:9) was more than likely the former slave of Philemon (as recounted in the New Testament book that bears his name). And Paul's overarching point to slave and master alike is that they are ultimately both servants of the universal Lord, Jesus Christ.

For slaves, their "earthly masters" are their lords "according to the flesh", meaning that their authority is limited to this world (3:22).[43] But their heavenly master, Jesus, is the international Christ and the Lord of heaven and earth, with unlimited authority. He is the one in, through and for whom all things were made. As you serve your earthly lord, remember that you are really serving your heavenly Lord. So fear Jesus. Serve Jesus. Work heartily for Jesus. And do it by serving the one whom Jesus has placed over you.

That means you will serve faithfully even when your earthly master can't see what you are doing. For unlike your earthly masters, Jesus can see everything. And Jesus cares about everything you do, which is why Paul finishes the chapter with these words: "For the wrongdoer will be paid back for the wrong he has done, and there is no partiality" (3:25).

To whom should we apply these verses? Too often,

43 In a footnote, the ESV gives "masters according to the flesh" as an alternative translation for "earthly masters".

interpreters jump straight to the employer-employee relationship that many of us experience in the West. But in so many parts of Asia, Africa and the Middle East, families have domestic servants to whom these verses will apply much more directly. I've even been in the homes of overseas missionaries who employ servants simply as part of the economic reality of those nations—to provide an income that those servants otherwise would never receive. Those servants are addressed directly by Paul's words: they are to work heartily, for the Lord.

Even in Western cultures, before we start thinking about employer-employee relationships, there are more direct applications to certain situations: for example, men and women in prison or those required to pay back debts through bonded scholarships (such as teachers or doctors). In each case, God says: work heartily, as for the Lord, and not for men—because you know that you will receive "the inheritance as your reward" (3:24).

Isn't that a wonderful thought? The slaves of Paul's day had no earthly inheritance. But as those united to Christ, God had qualified them to share in the heavenly inheritance of the saints in light. Isn't that incredible?

So God's good word to slaves commands them and enables them to obey their earthly masters sincerely and to work heartily, knowing that they are ultimately working for the Lord. And God's good word to masters commands and enables them to treat their slaves in a godly manner: "Masters, treat your bondservants justly and fairly, knowing that you also have a Master in heaven" (4:1). The way you treat your 'bondservant' should be a direct reflection of the way Jesus treats you.

I've seen this play out in the best possible way: a domestic servant in Dubai became a Christian because her "earthly masters" not only treated her justly and fairly but also treated her as one of their own, visiting her in hospital and (best of all) loving her enough to share the gospel with her. I understand that George Whitefield, despite his endorsement of slavery as an institution, shared the gospel with slaves and saw many of them converted, so much so that he had more slaves than white English people at his funeral.

So then, if these verses apply *directly* to the slave-master relationship, how much more should they apply *derivatively* to the employer-employee relationship? Employees, serve your earthly employer with sincerity of heart, fearing the Lord. Employers, treat your employees justly and fairly, knowing that you have a CEO in heaven.

In all of this, our first thought should not be for our own personal rights. In the disorder of our dark world, we understandably long for justice, equality and rights. But there's a certain irony in Christians pursuing their rights: Jesus, the beloved Son of God who was equal with God, willingly gave up his rights to die the death that we deserved. Surely that should give us some pause if we find ourselves prioritizing the pursuit of our rights above all else.

Yet at the very same time he was giving up his rights, Jesus was also reconciling all things to himself, bringing about true and peaceful order under his loving rule. We can rejoice and delight in the order that Christ has won for us. When lived out according to his good word to us, this God-given order is the wonderful fruit of the gospel—transforming our families, our churches, our workplaces and even whole societies.

Give thanks and pray

- Praise God that Jesus has reconciled all things to himself, bringing true order to our families, churches, workplaces and societies.
- Pray that God would enable you to delight in this sense of order.
- Pray that God would enable you to live out this sense of order in your own relationships: in your home, your workplace, your church and your community.

Discussion questions

- Does Colossians 3:18-4:1 make you feel uncomfortable? If so, why?
- What submissive roles or aspects of submission do you find hard?
- How can you make submission a joy for yourself and for others?

A word to wives

By Jeanette Chin

Submission can be a controversial can of worms. In Australia, secular journalists have recently published concerns about the dangers of submission. They're right to do so.

When men and women submit to Christ, we give up our selfish rights and preferences, and voluntarily choose to live under his authority. He owns our lives and asks for total allegiance. If Christ were not trustworthy and abounding in compassion, grace, wisdom and goodness, this would be a precarious position indeed. But, thankfully, submission to Christ is the truest freedom, so we need not fear.

But in this sinful world, power is abused. Men and women in all kinds of positions of influence and leadership can use their position selfishly and sinfully, and victims become injured by heinous evil. As such, submission is a risky business.

So when Christ says, "Wives, submit to your husbands, as is fitting in the Lord", there are risks. Sometimes husbands are foolish and make bad decisions. Sometimes husbands are sinful and abuse their wives. God speaks very clearly about the latter. He hates violence, rage, fits of anger and the abuse of power (Ps 11:5; Prov 3:29; Gal 5:19-21; Mark 10:42-45). Such people will be punished most severely (Gal 5:21).

So what do we do?

Ephesians 5:22-33 is the extended parallel of Colossians 3:18, where the hidden mystery of marriage is unveiled. God designed earthly marriages to give a fore-taste of the sublime goodness of the eternal marriage between Christ and the church. As such, wives are to be like the church, modelling submission so that every-one has a better understanding of what it looks like for individuals to submit to Christ. Likewise, husbands are to demonstrate Christ's headship, modelling sacrifi-cial, selfless leadership so we better understand Christ's loving rule. We are to learn from each other.

I am very grateful to God for the blessing of a won-derful, Christlike husband. Richard insists on taking out the garbage every week, he cooks when I'm busy, he drives when I'm tired and he comforts me when I'm sad. Submitting to him is a wonderful joy that I don't take for granted. I received this undeserved blessing through the painful death of another. So I cherish it dearly, thanking God for this tangible expression of Christ and the gospel.

Yet despite this, in my sinfulness, I still fail. Sometimes I get tired and grumpy. Sometimes I'm impatient and irri-table. To my shame, sometimes I get angry when I feel my husband hasn't loved me exactly as I want him to, and in a desire for justice I punish him for it. But Colossians says, "Husbands, love your wives, and do not be harsh with them". Should Richard only love me when I'm kind and patient and in a good mood? This would be outrageous! Husbands, even if your wife is angry and emotional, please love her patiently—with compassion, kindness and humility. Assume she knows how undeserving she is.

Likewise, wives, even if your husband is disappointing, slow to initiate, and clumsy in his efforts, please respect him, patiently encourage him, and build him up with your words. Assume he knows his weaknesses and failings. He might feel trapped and unable to change himself. He may feel self-hatred and pity for his own inadequacies and sins, and know just how undeserving he is of your loyalty and grace.

Ephesians 5:33 is very helpful in all this. Insightfully, author Emerson Eggerichs says that respect is the heart of submission, and the biblical 'love language' for men. In general, where women want to be loved and cherished and adored, men want to be respected.[44]

But sometimes in our ungodliness, instead of respecting our husbands, wives can belittle, demean and demand. Sometimes it's easy for us to have a critical, complaining or controlling spirit, especially when there are differing preferences and opinions. While there's certainly a right place to disagree and discuss, and while there's certainly a right place to keep a safe distance from a violent or abusive husband, it honours God to do so with loving respect—not with superiority and stubbornness, not with a spirit of revenge or bitterness, but with "compassionate hearts, kindness, humility, meekness, and patience" (Col 3:12).

As you continue reflecting on Colossians 3:18, these questions might be helpful: Do you appreciate

44 See *Love & Respect: The Love She Most Desires; The Respect He Desperately Needs*, Thomas Nelson, Nashville, TN, 2004.

your husband's work and service? Do you admire his strengths (or even his efforts) to love? Do you praise his godly ideas and leadership? Do you honour his preferences and desires?

Respect is most foundational to the goodness of submission: Whatever his failings, how can you treat your husband with respect and build him up with your words? Perhaps do some homework. Ask him, "What makes you *feel* respected?" You never know—the answer may surprise you.

7 | Fellow workers in Christ

Thirty feet beneath the earth in strict isolation, not knowing a thing about what was happening in the world above, I expressed my concern for spreading the Gospel on all continents, my love toward the Communists, and my burning desire that they (along with those they oppressed) might be saved. Basically, I dreamt in that solitary cell about an international mission to the Communist world. It seemed the vain fantasy of a sick mind.[45]

So wrote Richard Wurmbrand, founder of Voice of the Martyrs, who spent 14 years in prison for proclaiming the international Christ—three of those years in solitary confinement. "I lived many years in an isolated subterranean prison cell, in timelessness, something akin to the weightlessness experienced by astronauts," he wrote elsewhere. "Just as they know no difference between heavy

45 Richard Wurmbrand, *Voice of the Martyrs Magazine*, January 2018, p. 2.

and light, I knew no distinction between past, present, and future."[46]

It's hard to imagine anything lonelier or more isolating. And when we read the New Testament, we can sometimes think that the apostle Paul, like Richard Wurmbrand, struggled alone. But this was far from the case. Paul had many co-workers—men and women who played a vital part in his role as the apostle to the nations. Let's meet some of them.

Tychicus and Onesimus

> Tychicus will tell you all about my activities. He is a beloved brother and faithful minister and fellow servant in the Lord. I have sent him to you for this very purpose, that you may know how we are and that he may encourage your hearts, and with him Onesimus, our faithful and beloved brother, who is one of you. They will tell you of everything that has taken place here. (4:7-9)

Paul sent Tychicus and Onesimus as his messengers to the Colossians, to inform the Colossians of his situation. They were, in effect, his 'prayer letter' in the flesh.

And isn't Tychicus just the kind of person you'd want to recruit as a fellow worker? He was a *beloved brother*, thoroughly converted, and part of Paul's new family in Christ. He was a *faithful minister*, trustworthy and dependable to accurately deliver not only the gospel, but also the latest

46 Richard Wurmbrand, 'Cross-Bearers of the King', *Living Bulwark*, vol. 79, April/May 2015 (viewed 27 December 2018): www.swordofthespirit. net/bulwark/april2015p8.htm.

information about Paul. And he was a *fellow servant*, a 'slave'. There was no hierarchy between Paul and Tychicus, but Paul recognized him as a fellow slave of Christ.

Paul also describes Onesimus as a *beloved brother*. 'Onesimus', meaning 'useful', was a common name for slaves. This man was literally a 'useful slave'. It's likely that he was the very same slave mentioned throughout the letter to Philemon. If so, how tactful, insightful and pastoral of Paul to describe his co-workers this way: Tychicus—the free man—is called a 'slave' of Christ; Onesimus—the slave of Philemon—is simply a fellow and beloved 'brother.'

If Jesus is your Lord, then we serve him as brothers and sisters in Christ. We are family. We are not a 'tribe'—a word I have often heard Christians use to describe like-minded believers from their own part of the world. There should be no tribalism among God's people. We may come from different churches, different denominations or different socio-economic backgrounds, but we are not just disparate tribes. We are family.

Remember that Jesus is in *all* Christians. He is in us, and he unites us at the deepest possible level, regardless of any human distinctions between us. There are times when we may not get along with each other perfectly and it can feel like an imperfect or dysfunctional family. But we are still family—raised with Christ.

Paul had Christian brothers and sisters who remained with him, but he sent Tychicus and Onesimus back to Colossae—probably in possession of this letter and Paul's letter to Philemon—even though he had never met the Colossians.

Jewish and Gentile fellow workers

Look how Paul describes Aristarchus, Mark and Jesus (also called Justus), three of his co-workers who remained with him: "These are the only men of the circumcision among my fellow workers for the kingdom of God, and they have been a comfort to me" (4:11). These are Paul's fellow *Jewish* Christians (hence the use of the term "men of the circumcision") and his co-workers in Christ. And what a team! Aristarchus, we're told, even went to prison with Paul. Small wonder that these men proved a great comfort to him.

Then there are Paul's *Gentile* Christian fellow workers, including Epaphras, Luke and Demas (4:12-14). We've already met Epaphras earlier in the letter: the one who had first proclaimed the gospel to the Colossians. According to Philemon 1:23, he had also been a fellow prisoner with Paul. This is real commitment—real gospel *fellowship*. This is not just the kind of 'fellowship' based around having a chat over morning tea; this is self-sacrificial conformity to a shared vision of ministry and a life-altering commitment to see the gospel go to the ends of the earth, even if it meant going to prison together. Look at how Epaphras is described:

> Epaphras, who is one of you, a servant of Christ Jesus, greets you, always struggling on your behalf in his prayers, that you may stand mature and fully assured in all the will of God. For I bear him witness that he has worked hard for you and for those in Laodicea and in Hierapolis. (4:12-13)

He had served, not only in Colossae, but also in neighbouring cities. And look at how he laboured! He struggled, fought and agonized in prayer for them—as Paul struggled for the Colossians and the Laodiceans (2:1). Like our Lord Jesus praying in the Garden of Gethsemane, Epaphras prayed for the Colossians.

And did you notice what he agonizingly prayed for? That they would "stand mature" and be "fully assured" of God's will. These same threads have run right throughout the letter. Back in 1:9, Paul shared that he and Timothy had not ceased to pray together that the Colossians would be "filled with the knowledge of [God's] *will*". And Paul summarizes the goal of his ministry in the memorable words of 1:28: "Him [Christ] we proclaim, warning everyone and teaching everyone with all wisdom, that we may present everyone *mature* in Christ".

Epaphras' prayer for the Colossians is wonderfully in line with God's infallible gospel strategy. And his passionate, agonizing prayer encourages me to lift my game in prayer: to pray for the spread of the gospel around the world, to pray that God's people would stand mature in Christ, to pray that missionaries and gospel workers would persevere in their work, and to pray steadfastly in line with God's will for the world and with full assurance of his will.

This is what Paul has in view back at the beginning of chapter 4: "Continue steadfastly in prayer, being watchful in it with thanksgiving" (4:2). Paul implored the Colossians to pray with resolve, purpose and determination. And he relied deeply on God's answers to their prayers in order for his ministry to bear fruit (4:3-4).

Hudson Taylor, the founder of the China Inland Mission in the 19th century, was a man who followed Paul's teaching on prayer. This is how his son and daughter-in-law described Taylor's commitment to prayer:

> After sleep at last had brought a measure of quiet, they would hear a match struck and see the flicker of candlelight which told that Mr. Taylor, however weary, was poring over the little Bible in two volumes always at hand. From two to four AM was the time he usually gave to prayer; the time when he could be most sure of being undisturbed to wait upon God. The hardest part of a missionary career, Mr. Taylor found, is to maintain regular, prayerful Bible study. 'Satan will always find you something to do,' he would say, 'when you ought to be occupied about that, if it is only arranging a window blind.'[47]

We shouldn't feel compelled to emulate a model that involves praying from 2am to 4am—there is nothing ungodly about getting a good night's sleep! But what we should emulate is the attitude of dependence on God, the willingness to lay aside other distractions and give ourselves to prayer. As Paul says, and as Hudson Taylor discovered, we must be "watchful" in prayer. This has an echo of the Lord Jesus' command in Mark 13:32-33:

> But concerning that day or that hour, no-one knows, not even the angels in heaven, nor the Son, but only the Father. Be on guard, keep awake. (Mark 13:32-33)

So obeying Paul's command will mean more than just literally staying awake. It will mean praying in the light of the

---

47 Dr and Mrs Howard Taylor, *Hudson Taylor's Spiritual Secret*, Moody, Chicago, 2009, pp. 238-9.

Lord's return. That kind of thinking—that attitude of seeking things that are above—will not only keep you awake; it will also drive you to wrestle in prayer and to agonize in praying for others. Paul was captivated by Christ because he saw Christ clearly, as did Epaphras and their whole mission team. They were captivated by the international Christ, reigning in heaven, and set to return one day. In the light of seeing Christ clearly, they also saw the world and its needs clearly, which moved them to pray.

Prayer for open doors

Paul also asked the Colossians to pray for him:

> At the same time, pray also for us, that God may open to us a door for the word, to declare the mystery of Christ, on account of which I am in prison—that I may make it clear, which is how I ought to speak. (4:3-4)

Paul asked the Colossians to pray that God might open a door—not a prison door so he could walk free, but the door of opportunity so he could declare the mystery of Christ, the gospel for Jew and Gentile alike. His greatest desire was to proclaim that Jesus is the international Christ, the Lord of all and the King of kings.

But back then, as now, people objected to this message. That's why Paul is in chains. Many of those in the Jewish community didn't want to hear his message and nor did many of the Gentiles. And yet, while still in prison, his deepest longing is for everyone to hear the gospel of free forgiveness through the atoning death of Jesus, in order that they may be saved and presented mature in Christ. And so he asks for their prayers—not only that God would provide an opportunity to declare this mystery, but for clarity in his declaration.

It seems there's a simple formula at work in gospel proclamation: as clarity increases, opposition increases—so much so that Paul went to prison for the sake of the gospel. And he was willing to stay there.

As we move into a time of increasingly strident secularism, the day may be approaching where Christians in the West face going to prison for the sake of the gospel. But even if we are thrown in prison, wouldn't it be wonderful to ask for prayer like Paul? Shouldn't we pray, even in that moment, that God would open a door for the word of the gospel to go out through us? Shouldn't we ask that, even if we're in chains, God would enable us to proclaim the gospel with clarity?

Whether we are in prison or not, the gospel-shaped life involves not just *talking*, but also *walking*: "Walk in wisdom toward outsiders, making the best use of the time" (4:5). Your 'walk' refers to your conduct, your behaviour—your way of life. And Paul says that your way of life should be geared towards outsiders in a way that is wise: "walk *in wisdom* towards outsiders".

To walk this way is to live a Christ-saturated, God-glorifying life that is distinctively oriented towards the salvation of outsiders. In this sense, our lives should share the very heartbeat of Jesus Christ himself. The life Paul is describing comes from a heart that is in sync with God's will to seek and to save the lost.

If we do not have a heart for the lost, it may be that we are among the lost. But given that you have read this far into this book, I assume it's very likely that you do have a heart for the lost. If that's the case, how will you make "the best use of the time"? How will you 'redeem the time'? We should be godly exploiters of time, and good stewards of our time, all for the sake of outsiders.

We must face the challenges head-on and work at being good stewards of our time as we seek to engage with outsiders. Don't sleepwalk through your relationships, but be intentional in both your prayers and in the ways you spend time with those who don't know Jesus as Lord. Think about the outsiders you're likely to meet. Think about family, or friends at university or school, or work colleagues, or parents on the sideline at sporting events. Some of my richest gospel conversations have been on the sideline at soccer matches (or at the barber's shop!).

Gracious, salty conversation

And when we exploit such time with outsiders, what should our conversation look like? "Let your speech always be gracious, seasoned with salt, so that you may know how you ought to answer each person" (4:6).

Our speech must always be *gracious*. While this more than likely refers to the manner in which you engage, there are also echoes of the content of your speech being grace-centred. Back in 1:6, Paul described the gospel as being "the grace of God in truth". As recipients of God's grace, we are now to bring God's grace to others—both in the content of our speech and the manner in which we deliver that content.

Furthermore, Paul says we should let our speech be "seasoned with salt".

What exactly does this mean? The word 'salt' is used in many different ways throughout the Scriptures.[48] But the immediate context is the best way to determine Paul's meaning in this verse. Remember, Paul is addressing "*how* you ought to answer each person". So the point of having speech "seasoned with salt" is that we should not be bland, boring and insipid in the way we speak. Rather, we should be provocative. After all, the gospel itself is highly provocative.

At the very least, Paul is encouraging us to invest time in thinking about our conversations. Do some homework. Ponder how you can be more attractive and provocative in the way you speak with outsiders. Make them thirst for something more. After all, anything seasoned with salt will make a person thirsty. Isn't that what Paul accomplished in the sermon recorded in Acts 17? Isn't that what the Lord Jesus accomplished with so many of his parables? To paraphrase the way that Mark Dever, an American pastor, explained it: You should want to make your friends feel as though their lives don't make sense because of some 'x-factor'. And that 'x-factor' is the gospel.[49]

Does your conversation contain anything 'salty'? Does it move beyond the latest sporting event or your favourite TV shows? When you invite unbelieving friends to your home for a meal, pray for them, then intentionally think about

48 For example, in Deuteronomy 29:23, the effect of salt was to render land infertile. In Judges 9:45, salt was used as a symbol of desolation. In Leviticus 2:13, grain offerings were to be seasoned with salt as a symbol of the eternal covenant with God. And in Matthew 5:13, Jesus calls his disciples "the salt of the earth" as a description of their distinctiveness.

49 From a sermon delivered at St Thomas' Anglican Church, North Sydney on 12 February 2013 (accessed 27 December 2018): www.st-thomas.org. au/podcast/exploiting-and-provoking/.

how you can move the conversation towards the gospel. That means knowing something about your friends—knowing what makes them tick.

When I think of intentionally gospel-centred speech, I think of my friends Steve and Barbara, who live two houses away from us. Steve and Barbara invited my wife and I, together with some of our neighbours, to their home for a Danish Christmas dinner. I had never heard of a Danish Christmas dinner, but we had a fantastic time. We sang carols, danced around a Christmas tree decorated with candles and even blew out the occasional candle when it started to burn the tree.

During dinner, Barbara pulled out a children's Bible and started reading to our neighbour's four-year-old son Hamish (and to everyone else) about the birth of Jesus. After a while, she invited my wife to take over the reading. Before you knew it, twelve people were sitting around listening to the Christmas story. Barbara had worked out how to share the gospel with outsiders.

As well as finding inventive ways to create opportunities, we need to know the gospel. We need to think through the implications of the gospel—not so we can answer every single question, but so we have the best possible chance to help others see Jesus clearly and so be captivated by him.

So how are you stewarding your time with outsiders? Prayer is a great place to start, so at the end of the chapter I'll encourage you to pray for at least two friends who don't yet know Jesus as their Lord and Saviour.

Luke and Demas

Let's return to Paul's fellow gospel workers, this time Luke and Demas: "Luke the beloved physician greets you, as does Demas" (4:14). Luke is the author of Luke's Gospel and the book of Acts. He also happens to be a doctor. In many ways, his writings—which are mostly geared towards Gentiles—are a case study in how to "walk in wisdom toward outsiders": the books of Luke and Acts are fantastic for evangelizing unbelievers.

Then there's Demas, who is also referred to in Paul's letter to Philemon (Phlm 1:24). We are told nothing about Demas, apart from the fact that he greets the Colossians. But, tragically, in 2 Timothy—probably the last letter that Paul ever wrote—we learn that Demas deserted Paul because he was "in love with this present world" (2 Tim 4:10). It seems he had been captured by the 'elements' of this world, by "philosophy and empty deceit".

Can a Christian fall away?

It's a perennial question: can a Christian fall away? What we know from the Scriptures are the following truths:

The very faith that saves us is a gift from God (Eph 2:8). When God brings us to faith, we are a new creation (2 Cor 5:17; Gal 6:15), born of the Spirit (John 3:6), united with Christ in his death (Rom 6:5) and raised with him (Col 3:1). None of these things, which are done by God, can be undone.

However, it's equally important to emphasize that we must take the Bible's warnings seriously (e.g. Matt 7:21-23; Heb 6:4-8). These warnings may be the very means by which God keeps his saved people walking in Christ, but they are still real warnings. In the end, the Bible doesn't answer the question

"Can a Christian fall away?" with a "Yes" or a "No"; it answers it with an emphatic "DON'T!"

Perhaps it is best to understand the experience of friends or family 'falling away' as those who are amongst the first three soils of the parable of the sower (Matt 13:1-23).

We can't always pick who will be taken captive. People may look totally committed to Jesus and his gospel, and may even believe themselves to be totally committed, only to be led astray by the hollow and deceptive philosophies of the world. Out of all the hardship and suffering that Paul endured in gospel ministry, I suspect that nothing hurt him more than seeing fellow workers desert him and desert the Lord.

It may be that, like me, you've seen this happen to friends and it's caused you great pain. I think of one young man who used to meet with me every week to read the Bible. He was highly intelligent and committed to gospel ministry, and even went on to leave his home country to serve Jesus as a missionary. But while he was on the mission field, he abandoned the faith. It was heartbreaking. There is nothing more painful than to see someone you love walk away from Jesus—appearing to have received Jesus as Lord for a time, but then failing to walk in him.

However, at the time Paul wrote the letter to the Colossians, this group of Jewish and Gentile believers comprised the team that was with him, sharing the same concerns and bearing one another's burdens. Together, they sought to present everyone mature in Christ. But Paul also had fellow workers outside Colossae:

> Give my greetings to the brothers at Laodicea, and to Nympha and the church in her house. And when this letter has been read among you, have it also read in the church of the Laodiceans; and see that you also read the letter from Laodicea. And say to Archippus, "See that you fulfil the ministry that you have received in the Lord." (4:15-17)

Clearly, Paul intended this letter to be read not only by the Colossian church, but also in churches in surrounding cities. This suggests that much of the content of the letter is not specific to the Colossians. Many commentators devote their attention to identifying the 'Colossian heresy': what precise 'deceit' did Paul have in mind? But given that he speaks in general terms, and given that he intended this letter to be studied by other churches, it seems to me that there may not have been a specific 'Colossian heresy' at all. Rather, he is issuing general warnings that are applicable to all Christians—including us. The warnings against false teaching, the exhortation to set our minds on things above and the commands about how we walk towards outsiders are for all Christians.

We can go one step further. Given Paul's expectation that his writings should be read, studied and obeyed by multiple churches, it seems reasonable to conclude that Paul was self-consciously writing *Scripture*. That is, he doesn't simply understand his writings to be encouragement or even 'godly wisdom' from one Christian to a group of other Christians. Rather, he sees himself writing with the authority of the Lord himself—an authority that's in keeping with his role as Jesus' commissioned apostle to the nations.[50]

Whatever the case, Paul singles out Archippus and exhorts him to fulfil his God-given ministry. Presumably, this brother was a member of one, not all, of the churches that would be reading this letter. But now every church that reads the letter knows that Archippus has been charged to fulfil a vital role. Imagine your pastor singling you out in the church bulletin: "Richard, make sure you fulfil your role on the lawn-mowing roster". Now everyone will be watching! Paul apparently believed that a public exhortation and encouragement would help Archippus to persevere in gospel ministry.

What we have in these greetings, then, is Paul's list of fellow workers in the cause of Christ. Whether they are by his side or far away, and whether or not they had even met him, they share the same vision, the same dreams, the same passion and the same task: **the prayerful proclamation of Jesus to all the nations through suffering**.

If you are a Christian today, no matter where you live or how long you've been following Jesus, you have a part to play in this task. Your part may be large—the kind of ministry

---

50 cf. 1 Corinthians 2:7-13; 7:12, 25, 40; 14:37-38. Regarding Paul's expectation that the Colossians would read "the letter from Laodicea", it is quite possible that this actually refers to Ephesians. Note that Colossians 4:16 says "the letter *from Laodicea*" (not "the letter *to the Laodiceans*") and that many early manuscripts of Ephesians do not have the words "in Ephesus" in Ephesians 1:1 (suggesting that Ephesians may have been a 'circular letter'). Paul wrote both letters around the same time, probably around 62 AD while in Rome. See Lionel Windsor, *Reading Ephesians & Colossians*, p. 81, and 'Colossians 4:16—What happened to the Laodiceans?', *Defending Inerrancy* (viewed 27 December 2018): defendinginerrancy.com/bible-solutions/Colossians_4.16.php.

that reaches thousands. Or, like most of us, your part may be small—barely noticeable, perhaps even insignificant in most people's eyes. But if you are faithfully playing your part in God's strategy to save his people and glorify his Son, there is *nothing* insignificant about that. The fruit of your labour may only be seen in eternity, but it will be seen—and it will glorify Jesus. Paul knew that this God-given strategy was a team effort, undertaken by Christians who shared the same vision and passion for the salvation of the world.

Remember Paul's chains

As we come to the end of this magnificent, majestic letter, Paul gives one final command: "remember my chains" (4:18).

Why does Paul urge them to remember his chains? Given everything else he's said throughout the letter, it's unlikely that this is primarily about simply remembering that he is in prison, nor is it just a plea for sympathy. It may be that he is reminding them again to pray for his situation—not so much that he is released (an open door out of prison) but that he has opportunities to preach Christ (an open door for evangelism, as in 4:3).

But I suspect that Paul's primary concern is that they remember *why* he was in chains. That is, this is part and parcel of him "filling up what is lacking in Christ's afflictions for the sake of his body, that is, the church" (1:24). He suffers for the sake of the Colossians and the Laodiceans and all the Gentiles—ultimately for the sake of every person, in order to present them mature in Christ. He is primarily asking them to remember what his chains *symbolize*. Paul's chains symbolize God's infallible strategy: one last time, the prayerful proclamation of Jesus to all the nations through suffering.

Earlier in chapter 4, Paul urges us to make "the best use of the time" (4:5). If this is God's infallible strategy for the salvation of the world, then surely to be part of this strategy is the *very best* use of our time. That's why he wants them to remember his chains.

As you continue to walk in Christ, as you seek the things that are above, as you put to death whatever is earthly in you, as you put on the virtues of Christ, as you foster true order in all your relationships, as you walk in wisdom towards outsiders and as you play your part as a fellow worker in the gospel: *remember*.

Remember Paul's chains.

Give thanks and pray

- Praise God that he not only saves us in Christ, but that he also invites (and commands) us to be fellow workers in the gospel.
- Pray that God would enable you to continue steadfastly in prayer and to be watchful in it.
- Pray that God would open doors for you to proclaim Jesus and to be a faithful 'fellow worker' in your situation.
- Write down the names of at least two people who don't yet know Jesus as their Lord and Saviour. Thank God for these friends. Pray that God would help you to steward your time well and to share the gospel with them one way or another. Pray that God would save them.

Discussion questions

- How can you, like Epaphras, nurture habitual prayer for your *believing* family and friends (4:12)?
- How can you nurture habitual prayer for your *unbelieving* family and friends? How will you intentionally "walk in wisdom toward" them?
- How will you prayerfully "remember Paul's chains"?

Appendix:
The Colossians memory challenge

*W*hen I first began working on the talks that formed the backbone of this book, I made it my goal to memorize all of Colossians. I formed a group of three with two university students to read through Colossians and we decided, "Why not go all the way and memorize the whole book as well?"

Our approach was very simple: we started at the beginning of Colossians and tried to memorize a few more verses between our weekly meetings. Then we'd go back to the beginning and revise. Each time we met, we'd simply see how far we could go. By the middle of the year, we had essentially memorized the book word-for-word, so we simply kept reinforcing our work by seeing whether we could still say it aloud all the way through each time—hoping that we could still remember it all by the end of the year.

Based largely on Andrew Davis's book *An Approach to*

Extended Memorization of Scripture,[51] here are some ideas that might help you to tackle this hugely rewarding task. First, consider why it's worthwhile to invest time in this pursuit. Don't jump in too quickly, as this certainly requires a real investment of time. But ponder the benefits of memorizing a larger section of Scripture and address any excuses head-on (for example, if you think it will take too much time, do you need to address your priorities?).[52] Meditate on the psalmist's words in Psalm 119:9-11:

> How can a young man keep his way pure?
>> By guarding it according to your word.
> With my whole heart I seek you;
>> let me not wander from your commandments!
> I have *stored up your word in my heart*,
>> that I might not sin against you.

Davis recommends "surveying the terrain" before you begin: count the verses in your book, plan how many verses you can memorize each week, determine a possible finishing date, then add 10 per cent "so as not to feel under tremendous pressure until you get used to this lifestyle".[53] In the case of Colossians, there are 95 verses in our English Bibles. If you set the target of memorizing six verses a week, this will take 16 weeks. Adding ten percent would round this up to 18 weeks.

---

51 Andrew M Davis, *An Approach to Extended Memorization of Scripture*, Ambassador International, Greenville, SC, 2014.
52 Davis, 'Overcoming Excuses for not Memorizing' in *An Approach to Extended Memorization of Scripture*.
53 Davis, 'Surveying the Terrain' in *An Approach to Extended Memorization of Scripture*.

Davis also gives a range of practical tips, including the priority of retaining old verses before moving on to new ones, memorizing verse numbers as well as words, and "photographing the verses with your eyes". He also offers advice on how to retain the book over the long haul.

One of the great benefits of memorization is that you'll start to notice repeated words and ideas. Even though I'd studied Colossians and given various talks on it before, common words and the threads of ideas running through the letter suddenly became much clearer as I memorized the letter. For example, the concept of reconciliation in chapter 1 emerged as being very significant.

As another example, I noticed that the challenging section of chapter 3 that people find a little harder to take on board in the current climate—around wives submitting to husbands as is fitting in the Lord—all flows out of the context of "order in Christ". This concept actually begins right back in chapter 1, where we learn that it refers to Christ-saturated order. In chapter 2, Paul rejoices in seeing their "good order" (2:5) and he returns to it in chapter 3 by discussing order in the household. It was lovely to see those ideas coming through and I'm sure memorizing the letter helped me find the connections.

In the end, though, the real ongoing benefit of memorizing a letter like Colossians is simply to store up Scripture in your heart. We give ourselves to memorizing Scripture so we can meditate on it, live by it, rejoice in it, and stop sinning.

❀matthiasmedia

Matthias Media is an evangelical publishing ministry that seeks to persuade all Christians of the truth of God's purposes in Jesus Christ as revealed in the Bible, and equip them with high-quality resources, so that by the work of the Holy Spirit they will:

- abandon their lives to the honour and service of Christ in daily holiness and decision-making
- pray constantly in Christ's name for the fruitfulness and growth of his gospel
- speak the Bible's life-changing word whenever and however they can— in the home, in the world and in the fellowship of his people.

Our resources range from Bible studies and books through to training courses, audio sermons and children's Sunday School material. To find out more, and to access samples and free downloads, visit our website:

www.matthiasmedia.com

How to buy our resources

1. Direct from us over the internet:
   – in the US: www.matthiasmedia.com
   – in Australia: www.matthiasmedia.com.au

2. Direct from us by phone: please visit our website for current phone contact information.

3. Through a range of outlets in various parts of the world. Visit **www.matthiasmedia.com/contact** for details about recommended retailers in your part of the world.

4. Trade enquiries can be addressed to:
   – in the US and Canada: sales@matthiasmedia.com
   – in Australia and the rest of the world: sales@matthiasmedia.com.au

Register at our website for our **free** regular email update to receive information about the latest new resources, **exclusive special offers**, and free articles to help you grow in your Christian life and ministry.

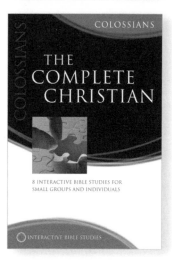

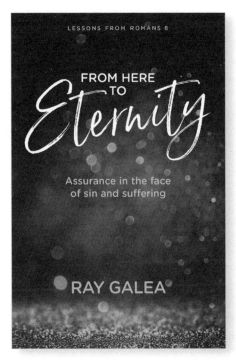